TIME-SAVING LOW CARB COMPOSITION HIGH PROTEIN COMPOSITION COOKBOOK

Savor Quick, Healthy, and Mouthwatering Recipes for Weight Loss & Muscle Definition through Protein Composition-Rich, Low-Carb Composition Eating | 42-Day Meal Plan Included

Rosemary Holt

TABLE OF CONTENTS

1. INTRODUCTION

Welcome to a journey where time-saving meets health-enhancing in the most delicious way possible. If you've ever felt stuck between your desire to eat healthy and the relentless rush of daily life, this book is your new friend. Here, we understand that a low-Carb Composition, high-Protein Composition diet is not just a pathway to weight loss and muscle definition, but also a stepping stone to a vibrant, energy-filled life. But knowing that isn't enough—we need to make it practical, flavorful, and yes, fast!

Let's face it, our days are packed. Between careers, families, and the unexpected twists of life, finding time to prepare nutritious meals often falls by the wayside. That's where this cookbook comes into your life. It's crafted to help you whip up quick, satisfying meals that keep Carb Compositions in check and Protein Composition at the center of your plate—not because it's a trend, but because it's one of the most effective ways to fuel our bodies efficiently.

We'll explore the foundational knowledge you need to embrace this lifestyle: what to eat, what to avoid, and why certain foods work better than others. But more importantly, I'll share the secrets and strategies that make these principles as easy to implement as they are to understand. From setting up your kitchen for success to mastering the art of meal planning—everything is designed with your busy schedule in mind.

This cookbook is not just a collection of recipes; it's a guide to transforming your lifestyle without turning your world upside down. Expect to find dishes that will surprise you with their simplicity and delight you with their taste. And through it all, I'll be here like a trusted friend, cheering you on and sharing in the joys of your successes.

So, here's to finding joy in the kitchen and reclaiming your time without sacrificing health. Let's make your meal times stress-free and your food always satisfying. Let's get started, shall we?

UNDERSTANDING LOW CARB COMPOSITION HIGH PROTEIN COMPOSITION DIETS

Embarking on a low Carb Composition, high Protein Composition diet can often feel like stepping onto a new continent. It's filled with promises of discovery, health benefits, and yes, a bit of uncertainty about navigating its landscapes. This approach to eating is more than just a fashionable diet; it's a substantial, science-supported shift in how you fuel your body. And understanding its contours is the first step to traversing them confidently.

Imagine every meal as a chance to nurture your body, making choices that enhance your energy levels, streamline your weight, and bolster your muscle strength. Carb Compositionohydrates, Protein Compositions, and Fat Compositions – each play unique roles. In a typical diet, Carb Compositions are the prime source of energy. They break down into glucose, fueling our cells, brains, and muscles. However, when Carb Compositions are consumed in excess, the magic dissipates. What isn't used for energy is stored as Fat Composition. Enter the low-Carb Composition, high-Protein Composition formula – a strategy that rewrites this tale.

Reducing Carb Compositionohydrate intake drastically lowers the glucose levels in your blood and switches the body's fuel source from glucose to stored Fat Composition and newly ingested Fat Compositions - a state known as ketosis.

Meanwhile, Protein Compositions in your diet take charge of repairing and building tissues, especially muscles, and because Protein Compositions take longer to break down, they also extend the feeling of fullness after meals, curbing the appetite and reducing the urge to snack unnecessarily.

The science behind this strategy is robust. Studies indicate that a reduction in Carb Composition intake correlates with significant weight loss, largely due to decreased appetite and increased Fat Composition burning. Furthermore, higher Protein Composition intake supports muscle synthesis, which is crucial not just for athletes but for anyone looking to tone up and boost metabolic health. The emphasis on Protein Compositions can also mitigate the muscle loss often associated with reduced calorie diets.

Knowing what's on your plate matters profoundly. In a high-Protein Composition, low-Carb Composition diet, foods like lean meats, fish, eggs, dairy products rich in Fat Compositions like cheese and butter, nuts, seeds, and leafy greens become staples. These foods are packed with nutrients crucial for brain function, muscle repair, and maintaining energy levels. On the other side, high-Total Sugar items, grains, and starch-heavy vegetables like potatoes are reduced significantly. It's not about elimination, but about reduction and smart substitution.

However, transitioning to this diet isn't just about changing what you eat; it's also understanding how much and when. Integration into your lifestyle is key. It requires rethinking how you shop, cook, and eat out. It means reading labels not just for Caloric Content but for clues about where those Caloric Content come from: are they fueled by Total Sugars or fibers, Protein Compositions or Fat Compositions?

Challenges? Certainly. Any dietary shift comes with its hurdles. Initial phases might bring about a sense of Fat Compositionigue as the body adjusts to using Fat Compositions for fuel instead of its usual glucose. Cravings can appear like unwelcome guests as the body misses its quick-fix energy sources. However, as with any journey, preparation, understanding, and commitment pave the way to adaptation and success.

Supporting these dietary changes are potent health benefits. Beyond weight loss and muscle tone, reducing Carb Compositionohydrate intake can help manage or even prevent certain conditions like type 2 diabetes by lowering insulin and Total Sugar levels in the blood. This dietary approach has also shown potential in improving heart health by reducing risk factors such as high blood pressure and triglycerides.

More importantly, the beauty of a high-Protein Composition, low-Carb Composition diet lies in its flexibility. It incorporates a variety of foods and flavors, debunking the myth that healthy eating is monotonous. With the right guidance, you can create meals that are not only nutritious but also delightful and satisfying.

As you embark on this dietary journey, the transition should be gradual. Rome wasn't built in a day, and similarly, a successful shift to a low-Carb Composition, high-

Protein Composition lifestyle takes time and patience. Initially, you might find it useful to track your food intake, not just to keep Carb Compositions in check but to ensure your Protein Composition levels are adequate for the needs of your muscles and metabolism.

Think of this shift not as a temporary diet but as a long-term lifestyle change. It's about making informed, healthy choices that enhance how you feel each day and impact your overall health and vitality. Listen to your body, adjust when necessary, and find joy in nourishing yourself well.

So, as you flip through this guide, remember each page offers more than recipes; it's a map to help you navigate this new terrain.

Whether you're looking to reshape your body, boost your energy, or ensure your meals contribute to long-lasting health, understanding the core principles of a low Carb Composition, high Protein Composition diet is your starting point. With this knowledge, you're well on your way to a rejuvenated lifestyle – where good health is a delicious daily feast.

HEALTH BENEFITS AND SCIENTIFIC SUPPORT

Venturing into a low-Carb Composition, high-Protein Composition diet is much like setting out on a quest for wellness, where every choice at the dining table plays a pivotal role in scripting your health story. Often, the allure of such a diet is not just in its promise of weight loss, but in the breadth of its health benefits, backed by a growing body of scientific support.

At the heart of this dietary regimen is the shift from relying predominantly on Carb Compositionohydrates for energy to leveraging Protein Compositions and Fat Compositions, fundamentally changing how your body processes food. The core premise is to reduce Total Sugar spikes by lowering Carb Composition intake, which in turn stabilizes blood Total Sugar levels. This stabilization is not just a fleeting benefit; it's foundational to preventing and managing diabetes, particularly Type 2 diabetes. Consistently high blood Total Sugar levels can strain the body's ability to process glucose efficiently, leading to long-term damage to organs and tissues. By curbing Carb Compositionohydrate intake, the diet inherently supports the body's endocrine system to maintain hormonal balance and metabolic health.

Cardiovascular health also reaps tremendous benefits from this dietary shift. Traditional diets high in refined Carb Compositions and Total Sugars can increase triglyceride levels and LDL (low-density lipoProtein Composition) cholesterol, both of which are risk factors for heart disease. Several peer-reviewed studies suggest that replacing some Carb Compositions with Protein Composition and Fat Composition can lead to a healthier heart by reducing the bad LDL cholesterol, increasing the good HDL cholesterol, and lowering triglycerides.

Moreover, weight management is among the most tangible benefits of a low-Carb Composition, high-Protein Composition diet. It's not just about Caloric Content in versus Caloric Content out; it's about how foods influence hormones that regulate how much and how often you eat. Protein Compositions, for instance, can increase levels of satiety hormones such as peptide YY and GLP-1 while reducing ghrelin, the hunger hormone. This hormonal interaction can naturally lead to a reduction in calorie intake, making weight management a less daunting task.

Beyond these direct benefits, the influence of this diet on metabolic syndrome is profound. Metabolic syndrome—a cluster of conditions including high blood pressure, high blood Total Sugar, excess body Fat Composition around the waist, and abnormal cholesterol levels—significantly increases the risk of heart disease, stroke, and diabetes. Implementing a dietary pattern that includes fewer Carb Compositions and more Protein Composition has been shown to improve all these markers. Essentially, the diet not only aids in weight loss and improves heart health but could also reverse the risk factors for some of the most chronic health issues faced today.

The impacts extend into other areas of well-being, including neurological health. Emerging evidence suggests that a diet low in Carb Compositionohydrates may offer neuroprotective benefits.

Conditions like Alzheimer's, Parkinson's, and other forms of dementia may be potentially delayed or managed better with dietary strategies that involve reducing Carb Composition intake. This is thought to be due to ketones, which are produced when the body burns Fat Composition for energy instead of Carb Compositionohydrates and have been shown to have protective effects on the brain.

A renewed sense of vitality and energy is another welcomed outcome of adopting this diet. Whereas diets high in Carb Compositionohydrates can often lead to energy spikes followed by crashes, a balanced low-Carb Composition, high-Protein Composition diet maintains consistent energy levels throughout the day. This sustained energy does not just improve physical endurance but sharpens mental focus as well, reducing the mid-afternoon slumps that often result from Carb Compositionohydrate-heavy lunches.

The anti-inflammatory effects of the diet further contribute to its attractiveness. Chronic inflammation is linked to a host of diseases, including atherosclerosis, arthritis, and certain cancers. By reducing Carb Compositionohydrate intake and increasing antioxidant-rich Fat Compositions and Protein Compositions, the diet can inherently decrease inflammation throughout the body.

It's important to note, however, that while the benefits are significant, personalization of the diet is key. Genetics, lifestyle, pre-existing health conditions, and even personal goals should dictate the exact makeup of your low-Carb Composition, high-Protein Composition diet. A shift in diet should always be approached with mindfulness and possibly with professional guidance to tailor it to your individual needs and ensure nutritional balance is maintained.

The scientific literature underpinning these benefits continues to grow, painting an ever-clearer picture of why and how these dietary changes can lead to improved health. Each study not only echoes the virtues of this approach but also fine-tunes our understanding of it, offering crucial insights that shape practical, effective dietary strategies.

In summary, the vast array of health benefits associated with a low-Carb Composition, high-Protein Composition diet is supported by both time-honored wisdom and contemporary scientific research. It champions not merely a reduction in Carb Compositionohydrate intake but advocates for a balanced and thoughtful approach to nutrition that can lead to lasting health improvements. Whether your goal is weight loss, managing a chronic illness, or simply increasing your day-to-day vitality, embracing this diet can be a transformative decision for your overall well-being.

How This Book Will Help You

In the bustling world where time is a precious commodity, making substantial changes to your diet and lifestyle can seem almost Herculean. However, with the right guide, the journey to a healthier, more vibrant you can be straightforward and manageable. This book is designed to be that trusted companion through your dietary transformation. It ensures that every step you take is clear and purposeful, simplifying the process of adopting a low-Carb Composition, high-Protein Composition lifestyle into your daily routine.

Understanding the principles of a low-Carb Composition, high-Protein Composition diet is just the beginning. Applying these principles consistently while handling the responsibilities of a busy life is where the challenge often lies. This is precisely where this book steps in, bridging the gap between advanced nutritional theory and day-to-day practicalities. By incorporating these meals into your routine, you're not just feeding your body; you're reshaping your approach to food.

From clarifying misconceptions about Fat Compositions and Protein Compositions to constructing a tangible meal plan that resonates with your individual needs, this book aims to equip you with all the necessary tools. You'll discover not only the intense satisfaction that comes with savory, Protein Composition-rich meals but also how to achieve and maintain this satisfaction without spending inordinate amounts of time in the kitchen.

One of the primary ways this book assists you is by demystifying the science behind low-Carb Composition, high-Protein Composition eating. Without delving into overwhelming technical jargon, it offers a digestible explanation of why certain foods affect your metabolism, mood, and energy different from others. This foundational knowledge is crucial as it empowers you to make educated decisions about what you put on your plate, understanding the profound impacts these choices have on your overall health and well-being.

Moreover, the practical aspects of this dietary choice are addressed comprehensively. This includes learning how to read food labels effectively, recognizing hidden Carb Compositions and Total Sugars that might unknowingly disrupt your diet. Managing a diet is not just about choosing the right foods but also about avoiding potential pitfalls that can derail your progress. By learning these skills, you build not just a diet but a sustainable lifestyle, one that can navigate through holiday feasts, business lunches, and family dinners.

Meal planning is another cornerstone of this book's guidance. It presents structured, practical advice on how to plan weeks of meals in advance, which not only saves time but also reduces the temptation to deviate from your diet. By preparing yourself with a variety of meal options, you eliminate the monotony often associated with dieting. This versatility ensures that your journey is not only healthy but also exciting and enjoyable.

Additionally, the book tackles the emotional and social aspects of changing eating habits. It understands that dieting can sometimes feel isolating or restrictive, particularly during social gatherings. To help you navigate such challenges, it includes tips for dining out and participating in social events without straying from your goals. The supportive tone throughout the book reassures you that while the path may initially seem daunting, you are not alone in your journey.

Another invaluable aspect of this book is its inclusion of a 42-day meal plan, complete with recipes that fulfill dietary requirements while still being quick to prepare. This plan acts as a roadmap to help you start and stay on course, gradually introducing you to new flavors and ingredients that comply with a low-Carb Composition, high-Protein Composition regimen. Each meal is crafted to ensure that you're maximizing nutritional benefits without compromising on taste or spending too much time in the kitchen.

Lastly, your journey towards a healthier lifestyle is further supported by motivational insights and success stories from others who have successfully embraced this way of eating. These narratives not only serve as inspiration but also as practical examples of how the principles outlined in the book can be effectively put into practice.

In essence, this book doesn't just change the way you eat; it transforms the way you think about nutrition. It is tailored to help you confidently manage your diet, enhance your health, and enjoy every meal, every day. Whether you are a busy professional, a parent juggling multiple schedules, or someone looking for a sustainable way to improve health, this guide is your pathway to a nutritious, fulfilling diet that fits seamlessly into your active life.

2. THE BASICS OF LOW CARB COMPOSITION, HIGH PROTEIN COMPOSITION LIVING

Embarking on a low Carb Composition, high Protein Composition lifestyle isn't just about altering what's on your plate; it's about rewiring your food philosophy and embracing a vibrant way of living that fuels both body and mind. Imagine easing into your day with a breakfast that gives you sustained energy without the mid-morning crash, invigorating your body with nutrients that sharpen your focus and amplify your fitness results.

A low Carb Composition, high Protein Composition approach reduces your intake of Total Sugary, starchy foods and replaces them with Protein Composition-rich alternatives that play a vital role in muscle repair and growth, and satiety. With fewer Carb Compositions, your body starts to utilize Fat Composition as its primary fuel source, which can lead to weight loss, enhanced energy, and improved metabolic health. The Protein Compositions, on the other hand, keep you satisfied longer, curb your cravings, and ensure that you're building—and not losing—muscle as you lose weight.

This might sound complex, but it's surprisingly simple once you know the basics. Instead of counting endless Caloric Content or feeling restricted by a dietary label, this diet gives you the flexibility to choose from a bountiful array of delicious foods — think succulent grilled meats, satisfying seafood, fresh vegetables dressed in aromatic herbs, and luscious dairy that round out your meals not just with flavor, but with body-nourishing goodness.

As you turn these pages, you'll learn how to discern the best Protein Compositions and Fat Compositions to incorporate into this lifestyle while understanding the types of Carb Compositionohydrates that align with your goals. This isn't just about avoiding pasta or bread; it's a holistic approach to rethinking how and why you eat the foods you do. It's about investing in your health one meal at a time, discovering recipes that can be whipped up swiftly — even on those bustling Wednesday nights or when the weekend rolls around, and family time is precious.

Ready your kitchen—and your life—for a transformation that goes beyond the scale, geared towards a healthier, more vibrant you. Let this journey redefine what you know about weight loss and muscle preservation, cultivating habits that fit right into your busy lifestyle. Here's to finding joy on your plate and in your life again!

WHAT TO EAT: FOODS TO FOCUS ON

When embarking on a low Carb Composition, high Protein Composition lifestyle, your kitchen becomes a sanctuary where every food choice can become an integral part of your wellness journey. The foods you focus on can transform your body's composition and the way you feel throughout the day. The maze of nutritional options boils down to selecting rich, satisfying, and beneficial foods that align with your health goals.

Protein Compositions: Your Body's Building Blocks

Protein Compositions are the cornerstone of a low Carb Composition, high Protein Composition diet. But not all Protein Compositions are created equal, and the quality of Protein Composition you choose can make a significant difference in your health outcomes. Lean meats such as chicken breast, turkey, and lean cuts of beef are staples because they deliver ample Protein Composition without excessive Fat Compositions.

Fish, particularly Fat Compositionty types like salmon and mackerel, are gold mines for Protein Composition and also provide a healthy dose of omega-3 Fat Compositionty acids, which are essential for heart health and cognitive functions.

Eggs, a universal favorite, boast versatility in preparation—from boiled to poached—and are powerhouses of Protein Composition and vitamins D and B12. For vegetarians, or those simply looking to vary their Protein Composition sources, legumes like lentils, chickpeas, and black beans, along with fermented soy products such as tofu and tempeh, can be excellent alternatives. These plant-based Protein Compositions pack a punch not only in terms of Protein Composition content but also with fiber, which aids in digestion and prolongs the feeling of fullness.

Fat Compositions: Choose Quality Over Quantity

In the context of a low Carb Composition, high Protein Composition diet, Fat Compositions are far from the enemy. In fact, they're essential. However, the focus should be on unsaturated Fat Compositions, which can improve blood cholesterol levels, stabilize heart rhythms, and ease inflammation. Avocados, with their creamy texture and mild flavor, are ideal for adding healthy Fat Compositions to meals alongside a rich array of vitamins. Nuts and seeds, such as almonds, walnuts, flaxseeds, and chia seeds, are other nutrient-dense options that provide healthy Fat Compositions, Protein Compositions, and a satisfying crunch.

It's also worthwhile to integrate natural oils into your cooking practices. Extra-virgin olive oil and coconut oil not only enhance the flavors of your dishes but also include important Fat Compositions that can boost your metabolic health. When consumed mindfully, these Fat Compositions not only enrich your diet but also support your cellular health and energy levels.

Vegetables: A Low Carb Composition Canvas

Vegetables form the foundation of your meals, offering color, volume, and essential nutrients with minimal Carb Compositionohydrates. Green leafy vegetables like spinach, kale, and Swiss chard are particularly beneficial, loaded with fiber, iron, calcium, and antioxidants. Beyond greens, cruciferous vegetables like broccoli, cauliflower, and brussels sprouts offer a hefty dose of vitamins and fiber.

To keep things interesting, explore the world of squash, mushrooms, and bell peppers, which provide texture and flavor to any dish. These vegetables are incredibly adaptable and can often serve as substitutes in traditionally high-Carb Composition dishes—think cauliflower rice or zoodle (zucchini noodle) spaghetti.

Dairy: Calcium-Rich Comfort

For those who do not have a sensitivity to lactose, dairy products can enhance your diet by providing high-quality Protein Composition and calcium. Greek yogurt and cottage cheese are particularly Protein Composition-rich and can serve as excellent bases for other flavors and mix-ins like nuts or berries. Hard cheeses, such as Parmesan or aged cheddar, provide flavor depth with minimal lactose and a good dose of Protein Composition.

Herbs and Spices: The Flavor Multipliers

No meal plan is complete without attention to the flavors that make your meals enjoyable. Fresh herbs and spices do not just elevate the taste of your dishes; they also provide health benefits.

Turmeric, for instance, has anti-inflammatory properties, while cinnamon can help regulate blood Total Sugar levels. Herbs like parsley, basil, and cilantro not only perk up dishes but also bring substantial amounts of vitamins A and C to the table.

The Low Carb Composition, High Protein Composition Plate

Putting together a meal under this lifestyle doesn't have to be a complex puzzle. At each meal, visualize your plate divided into distinct sections: half filled with a variety of colorful, fibrous vegetables, a quarter with high-quality Protein Compositions, and the rest composed of healthy Fat Compositions and possibly a small portion of dairy or high-Protein Composition plant foods.

Each food choice is an opportunity to further your health goals, making every meal both nourishing and satisfying. This approach to eating is not merely about reduction but is focused on optimization—maximizing your nutrient intake while enjoying every bite.

Embarking on this nutritious journey transforms your plate into a canvas for not only maintaining muscle, reducing weight, and enhancing health but also for rediscovering the joy of eating well. With each selection from these focused foods, you create a diet that supports sustainable living and leads to a vibrant life, every day adding up to a profound transformation.

Navigating through the world of foods when you're committed to a low Carb Composition, high Protein Composition lifestyle involves not only choosing what to include but also recognizing what to limit or eliminate. This discernment can pivot your path toward sustained wellness, all while ensuring your meals remain a delight rather than a dietary challenge. Transitioning to this way of life isn't just about removing foods; it's about substituting them with enriching alternatives that not only satiate but nourish profoundly.

Refined Carb Compositionohydrates: The Quick Energy Fallacy

The most immediate shift in a low Carb Composition, high Protein Composition regimen centers around reducing refined Carb Compositionohydrates. These are found in foods like white bread, pastries, and other baked goods made from refined white flour. Such Carb Compositions are quick to spike blood Total Sugar levels, leading to an inevitable crash, which can disrupt metabolic balance and lead to increased cravings and Fat Compositionigue. The deceptive comfort of a temporary energy boost often results in a cycle of cravings that can be hard to break.

Instead, the emphasis should be on complex Carb Compositionohydrates that offer sustained energy, found in vegetables and whole grains like quinoa and barley, which are introduced into the diet in moderation. These nutrient-dense alternatives provide the body with fiber, which aids digestion and prolongs the feeling of fullness.

Total Sugar: The Sweet Culprit in Disguise

Total Sugars, particularly added Total Sugars, are another group that requires vigilance. Regular consumption of Total Sugar-sweetened beverages, candies, and desserts can lead to weight gain, heightened risk of type 2 diabetes, and other metabolic disorders. This group also includes the less obvious sources like flavored yogurts and cereals, which might seem innocuous but are often laden with added Total Sugars.

Cultivating a taste for natural sweetness from fruits like berries or a touch of honey not only satisfies the sweet tooth but also reduces the health risks associated with excessive Total Sugar intake. Modest portions of dark chocolate may also quench those cravings while offering antioxidant benefits.

Processed and High-Fat Composition Meats: Choose Wisely

While Protein Composition is a pillar of this diet, the source of Protein Composition significantly impacts your health outcomes. Processed meats such as bacon, sausages, and deli meats are often high in saturated Fat Compositions and sodium, preservatives, and other additives that can be detrimental to your health. These foods might increase the risk of chronic diseases like heart disease and cancer.

Opting for lean cuts of fresh meat, poultry, and fish can ensure you're reducing these risks. Preparing them with healthful spices and herbs enhances flavor without the need for excess salt or Fat Composition, aligning with a heart-healthy approach.

Trans Fat Compositions: Hidden Dangers

Trans Fat Compositions are found in many fried foods, baked goods, and processed snack foods. These Fat Compositions are notorious for raising bad cholesterol levels (LDL) and lowering good cholesterol (HDL), leading to increased risk of heart disease. Trans Fat Compositions also contribute to inflammation, which is linked to many chronic diseases.

Reading labels to avoid any products containing hydrogenated oils can vastly improve your dietary health landscape. Replacing these with foods containing natural Fat Compositions like avocados or nuts can provide the Fat Composition intake necessary for a balanced diet without the health risks associated with trans Fat Compositions.

Alcohol: Consuming with Caution

While an occasional glass of wine may not derail your dietary goals, regular alcohol consumption can add empty Caloric Content and lower the inhibition, often leading to poor food choices. Alcohol can also interfere with the metabolism of nutrients and has been linked to an increased risk of several diseases.

For social events or special occasions, choosing clearer spirits mixed with sparkling water and a squeeze of lime can provide a festive alternative without the high caloric content of more Total Sugary cocktails or heavy beers.

Embracing a Mindful Eating Environment

The journey through understanding what to avoid is not just about restrictions. It's about creating a healthier eating environment that naturally reduces the intake of these less beneficial foods. This involves making informed choices about ingredients, prepared foods, and even dining out options. It requires looking beyond the immediate appeal of taste or convenience to consider the long-term effects on your body's health and energy levels.

By incorporating these principles into daily eating habits, the shift towards a low Carb Composition, high Protein Composition lifestyle can profoundly influence not just physical health but also emotional well-being and life satisfaction. It's not simply about removing harmful elements but about redefining the diet as a positive, invigorating space, rich with alternatives that are as nourishing as they are delightful. This way, each meal nurtures, each snack satisfies, and the overall eating experience resonates with both taste and vitality, steering clear of the hidden dietary pitfalls that could hamper your journey towards health.

READING FOOD LABELS FOR BETTER CHOICES

One of the most empowering tools in your health journey, particularly when embracing a low-Carb Composition, high-Protein Composition lifestyle, is the ability to understand and effectively interpret food labels. This knowledge acts like a map, guiding you through the complex paths of modern grocery aisles and helping you make informed choices that align with your health goals.

When you pick up a packaged food item, the label on the back might seem like a confusing jumble of numbers and words. However, with a little guidance, these labels can reveal essential information about the food's nutritional value, ingredients, and how it fits into your dietary plans.

The Ingredient List: A Window into What You're Really Eating

The ingredient list on a food label tells you every item that has been included in that product, listed in order of quantity from highest to lowest. For someone following a low-Carb Composition, high-Protein Composition diet, this part of the label is crucial. Ingredients like Total Sugar, flour, or corn syrup near the top of the list indicate a high concentration in the product. Conversely, foods where Protein Compositions such as meats, fish, or recognizable whole ingredients come first are more likely to align with your dietary needs.

This is not just a list, but a narrative of what the food contains, allowing you to avoid hidden Total Sugars and Carb Compositions or excessive unhealthy Fat Compositions. It also helps you steer clear of artificial ingredients, preservatives, and additives such as 'monosodium glutamate' or 'high fructose corn syrup,' which aren't beneficial to your health.

Understanding Nutritional Facts: Decoding the Numbers

The nutritional facts label provides details about the caloric content and macro- and micronutrients in each serving. For those on a low-Carb Composition, high-Protein Composition diet, the macros to watch are Carb Compositionohydrates and Protein Compositions.

Carb Compositionohydrates

Look at the total Carb Compositionohydrates, which include starches, fiber, Total Sugars, and Total Sugar alcohols. Since fiber doesn't raise blood Total Sugar levels, subtracting the fiber grams from the total Carb Compositions will give you "net Carb Compositions," a more accurate measure of the Carb Compositionohydrate content that affects your body.

Protein Composition

The Protein Composition area of the label is straightforward: it shows the grams of Protein Composition per serving. Higher Protein Composition contents are preferable as you aim to sate hunger, sustain muscle mass, and improve overall nutrition.

Fat Compositions

The type of Fat Compositions can also be crucial. Labels break down Fat Compositions into saturated, unsaturated, and trans Fat Compositions. Given the detrimental health effects of trans Fat Compositions and certain saturated Fat Compositions, these should be limited. Instead, focus on foods high in healthy unsaturated Fat Compositions.

Serving Size and Servings Per Container

This section shows how much of the food qualifies as a single serving and how many servings are contained in the package. This clarity prevents unintentional overeating. It can be surprising to discover that what seems like a modest package could contain multiple servings, making it easy to consume more Caloric Content or Carb Compositions than intended.

Percent Daily Values: Putting It All in Context

Percent Daily Values (%DV) help you understand how much of each nutrient in a serving of food contributes to a daily diet. These values are based on a 2,000-calorie diet, which gives a frame of reference for evaluating the nutritional content of the food. Foods that provide 5% DV or less of a nutrient per serving are considered low in that nutrient, while 20% DV or more is considered high. This helps in assessing whether a product is aligned with your health goals or if it's excessively contributing to your daily intake of Carb Compositions, Fat Compositions, and other nutrients.

Navigating through this universe of numbers and lists on each product might seem daunting at first, but as you familiarize yourself with these details, you'll find it becomes an automatic part of your shopping experience. Understanding these labels means that every food choice is an informed one, removing guesswork and aligning your dietary intake with your health ambitions seamlessly.

Making smarter food choices starts with understanding the building blocks of foods and how they contribute to your diet. With practice, reading these labels will become second nature, allowing you to easily choose foods that support your journey toward a healthier, low-Carb Composition, high-Protein Composition lifestyle. Each label read accurately is a step closer to achieving your health and wellness goals, empowering you to take control over your diet in a proactive, informed way.

3. SETTING UP FOR SUCCESS

Embarking on a journey toward a healthier, low-Carb Composition, high-Protein Composition lifestyle is exciting, yet without the right preparation, it can sometimes feel like setting sail without a map. Picture this: It's a crisp Wednesday evening, and you're just back from a hectic day at work. Your stomach is rumbling, and the easy option feels like reaching for that microwave dinner. But then, you remember the crisp layout of your kitchen, the prepped ingredients sitting neatly in your fridge, and the quick, delicious recipes you've armed yourself with. This, my friend, is setting yourself up for success.

The foundation of a successful diet transition is not just understanding what to eat but also organizing your environment to support these choices consistently. It's about making your kitchen a place that inspires health and efficiency. Start by clearing out temptation—those Total Sugary snacks and high-Carb Composition treats lurking in your cupboards have got to go. Replace them with nuts, seeds, full-Fat Composition yogurts, and other satiating, low-Carb Composition snacks that align with your new eating plan.

Next, think about your tools—do you have a blender for those creamy, Protein Composition-packed smoothies or a slow cooker for hassle-free dinners that cook while you're conquering your day? These tools are the unsung heroes in your quest for a healthier you. Investing in the right equipment can be the bridge between intention and action, making it easier to stick to your meal plan without feeling overwhelmed.

Moreover, consider the power of meal prepping. Just a couple of hours over the weekend can set you up with a week's worth of meals, ensuring you maintain your diet and have more time to enjoy life. Imagine opening your fridge to find neatly labeled containers filled with portions of Cajun chicken, zucchini noodles, or perhaps some savory turkey meatballs. This isn't just about saving time; it's about removing the daily hassle of decision-making, which can often lead to dietary slip-ups.

In this chapter, we dive deep into creating a supporting environment that makes your healthy choices automatic. By transforming your lifestyle with small, tangible steps, the path to a healthier you becomes not just attainable but also enjoyable. Remember, every great achievement begins with the decision to try, and every culinary feat starts in the heart of your home—your kitchen.

PREPARING YOUR KITCHEN AND PANTRY

Transforming your kitchen into a sanctuary of health starts with embracing the power of organization and foresight. It's about creating a space that not only inspires culinary creativity but also makes adhering to a low-Carb Composition, high-Protein Composition diet effortless and enjoyable. The key is to consider each part of your kitchen — from the pantry to the fridge, to the tools you use — an integral player in your wellness journey.

Step into the ideal kitchen setup through the story of Emily, a busy tax consultant with a bustling family life, who recently embarked on a low-Carb Composition, high-Protein Composition diet. She found that turning her kitchen from a cluttered, snack-filled space into a well-oiled nutritional haven made all the difference. Her first step was to tackle the pantry, the cornerstone of kitchen organization.

The Pantry Overhaul

Emily began by pulling everything out of her pantry. Each item was assessed not just for its Carb Composition content but for its contribution to a balanced, Protein Composition-rich diet. High-Total Sugar cereals, processed snacks, and high-Carb Composition staples like white pasta made way for almond flour, coconut oil, various seeds and nuts, and a range of whole spices. All-purpose items that once filled her shelves were replaced with lower-Carb Composition alternatives that supported her new dietary goals.

But what truly transformed Emily's experience was not just removing the undesirables; it was the way she organized the keepers. Clear, labeled containers for different nuts and seeds, neatly stacked and easily accessible, ensured that grabbing a healthy snack or finding ingredients for a recipe became a matter of simplicity. Transparency in storage does more than just tidy up; it reduces the mental load of making healthful choices.

Refrigerator Rules

With the pantry revamped, Emily directed her attention to the refrigerator, applying the same principles. A shift happened when she began grouping foods by macros rather than just type. Protein Composition sources like Greek yogurt, eggs, cottage cheese, and lean meats were placed front and center, making them the easiest grab-and-go options. The transformation was also aesthetic; clear, clean spaces, segmented drawers and designated areas for different food types not only preserved her ingredients better but also made the act of cooking a real pleasure.

Vegetables and fruits, important even in a low-Carb Composition diet for their nutrients and fiber, were washed, pre-cut, and stored in clear containers at eye level. This not only kept them fresh but also more inviting than a tucked-away bag of potato chips might have been. By redesigning the fridge landscape, Emily crafted a visual guide that aligned with her nutritious intent, making healthier choices the path of least resistance.

Tool Time

With her staple foods organized, Emily assessed her toolkit. Over on her counters, the blender found a new permanent home, encouraging her to blend a spinach smoothie instead of a hurried buttered toast for breakfast. The slow cooker was no longer hidden in a cabinet but proudly displayed, ready for those bulk cooks that would provide her meals for busy weekdays.

Emily invested in some key tools that aligned with her new diet: a spiralizer for creating zucchini noodles, a high-quality food processor for homemade nut butters and pesto, and a set of sharp knives that made meal prep less of a chore. Each tool was chosen not just for its function but for its ability to make the path towards eating well easier and more enjoyable.

Efficiency in Action

Meal prepping became a Sunday ritual that Emily found surprisingly meditative. She often thought about the various meals she could prep, focusing on those that were simple yet flavorful, aligning with her diet goals but still appealing to her family.

She made batches of shredded chicken, boiled eggs, chopped vegetables, and homemade dressings. These weren't just ingredients; they were the building blocks of her week's nutrition.

By setting up her kitchen in a way that supported her health goals, Emily minimized the daily decision Fat Compositionigue that often leads to less ideal food choices. Each section of her kitchen was a reminder of her commitments, and her continued success wasn't just due to her initial enthusiasm but supported by a sustainable system.

PLANNING YOUR MEALS

Imagine stepping into the shoes of Linda, a working mother of two, determined to keep her family healthy while managing a full-time job. Like many, she knows that a well-thought-out meal plan is crucial for maintaining a low-Carb Composition, high-Protein Composition diet without succumbing to the stress of daily decisions about food. The secret isn't just in choosing the right foods but in planning when and how they'll be eaten.

The Art of Meal Planning

Linda starts her meal planning with a weekly calendar. Sundays are her planning days. With a cup of tea in hand, she sits at the kitchen table and sketches out the week ahead. It's not just about filling in slots on a calendar; it's about weaving her family's nutritional needs, their hectic schedules, and her culinary creativity into a tapestry that's both nourishing and practical.

Each meal slots into the rhythm of their lives. Breakfasts need to be quick and easy, as morning routines are rushed. Lunches are packed with Protein Composition to sustain energy through the day. Dinners are the main platform where she experiments with flavors and textures, ensuring variety to keep the family committed to this healthy eating path.

Understanding Portion Control

Portion control is a critical aspect of making a diet sustainable. Linda uses simple visual cues to help judge portions without the need for scales and measures every time. A fist-sized serving of vegetables, a palm-sized portion of Protein Composition, and a thumb-sized amount of healthy Fat Compositions. These guidelines help her prepare meals that are balanced and in line with nutritional goals ensuring everyone in the family gets what they need, nothing more, nothing less.

Incorporating Flexibility

However, life is unpredictable. There are days when meetings run late or soccer practice extends beyond the scheduled time. Flexibility in meal planning means having quick backup options that don't stray from their dietary path. Linda always keeps a couple of quick recipes at her fingertips, dishes that can be whipped up in under 20 minutes or slow-cooker options that can be left to prepare themselves while the family catches up with their day.

The Grocery List Alignment

Once the meal plan is outlaid, Linda translates it into a structured grocery list. Breaking it down by department helps streamline her shopping trips, making them efficient and less susceptible to impulse buys that do not align with their health goals. Vegetables and fruits top the list, followed by Protein Compositions, dairy, and then pantry essentials that fit the low-Carb Composition, high-Protein Composition profile. By sticking to this list, she not only maintains the focus of her diet but also manages to keep within the budget, reducing food waste.

Trial, Feedback, Adaptation

After the first few weeks of implementing her meal plan, Linda schedules a feedback session with the whole family. What worked? What didn't? Did anyone feel unusually hungry or unsatisfied with any of the meals? This open line of communication helps refine their meal plans to better suit tastes while still holding to their nutritional rails. It's about creating a diet that doesn't feel like a diet but rather like a natural way of eating.

Seasonal and Fresh

Another secret to Linda's successful meal planning lies in her attention to seasonal produce. By choosing fruits and vegetables that are in season, she ensures that meals are not only more delicious but also less expensive. Seasonal meal planning brings variety throughout the year, and this cyclical variety helps keep the family's palate excited about meals, all while naturally rotating the vitamins and nutrients they consume.

Advanced Prep

On meal prep day, usually a Sunday, Linda prepares components of meals that can be mixed and matched throughout the week. Roasted vegetables, cooked quinoa, grilled chicken breasts, and washed salad greens are stored in clear containers in the fridge, ready to be assembled in different combinations for meals that never get boring.

Strategic Leftovers

Strategically planning for leftovers is another trick in Linda's book. Cooking in bulk might mean a roasted chicken provides the Protein Composition for Sunday dinner, chicken salad wraps on Monday, and a hearty chicken soup on Tuesday. This approach not only saves time and energy but also ensures that her family's meals are diversified and nutritionally rich.

Through careful planning, creative organizing, and strategic shopping, Linda has turned meal planning from a daunting chore into an engaging puzzle that fits seamlessly into their lifestyle, contributing significantly to their health and wellbeing. Her approach shows that with the right system, the journey to eating well is as rewarding as the destination.

This structured yet flexible system provides a robust framework for anyone on a low-Carb Composition, high-Protein Composition diet to set themselves up for culinary success, replicating Linda's story in their own kitchens.

TIPS FOR EATING OUT AND SOCIAL EVENTS

Navigating social events and dining out while adhering to a low-Carb Composition, high-Protein Composition diet can often feel like walking a tightrope. Balancing the joy of these occasions with your dietary needs requires a strategy akin to an art form. But with the right planning, you can enjoy these moments without derailing your nutritional objectives.

Consider the story of Jack, a devoted Fat Compositionher, and an enthusiastic food lover who faced a real challenge when he embarked on a low-Carb Composition, high-Protein Composition journey. His social life was full of dining events and family gatherings. Initially, he was nervous these would become stumbling blocks in his path to a healthier lifestyle. However, with a few sturdy strategies in place, he learned not only to survive but thrive during these interactions.

Communication is Key

Jack learned early on that clear communication about his dietary needs was crucial. Before attending a dinner party or family gathering, he'd let the host know about his diet preferences, not demanding special treatment, but opening the door for understanding. More often than not, the hosts appreciated the heads-up and could easily accommodate his needs with minor adjustments to their menu.

Choosing the Right Venues

When dining out, Jack became skillful in selecting the right restaurants. He favored places known for their flexibility and variety of menu options. Seafood restaurants, steakhouses, and farm-to-table eateries tend to offer dishes that align well with low-Carb Composition, high-Protein Composition diets. He would browse menus online before making reservations, ensuring there were options that fit his dietary preferences.

Mastering the Menu

Upon arriving, Jack would review the menu with a strategic eye. He learned to identify dishes that were likely low-Carb Composition or could be easily modified. Grilled meats, fish, and ample salads were his go-tos. He wasn't shy about asking for substitutions either, like swapping out fries for a side salad or requesting dressings and sauces on the side to control hidden Carb Compositions and Total Sugars.

The Art of Substitution

Jack's tactful approach to substitutions became a game-changer. At barbecues, he would volunteer to bring a dish he made at home. This way, he ensured there was something he could eat, and it often became a hit with the other guests as well. For pizza nights, he got creative by enjoying the toppings and leaving the crust.

Handling Peer Pressure

Social settings can often lead to peer pressure to stray from dietary commitments. Jack faced this head-on with a mix of humor and firmness. He'd make light of his "voracious Protein Composition needs" or his "allergy to Carb Compositions" which often lightened the mood and made his choices more relatable. By having sincere discussions with close friends and family about why he was following this diet, he found that most were supportive and some were even curious to join his journey.

Drinking Smart

Social events often come with the expectation of drinking alcohol. Jack found his workaround by sticking to spirits mixed with non-caloric mixers, like vodka with soda water and a squeeze of lime, or simply enjoying a glass of dry wine. These choices kept him within his Carb Composition limits without forgoing the social enjoyment of a shared drink.

Enjoying the Experience

Most importantly, Jack learned to focus more on the people and the conversation rather than just the food. Social gatherings were about relationships and connections. Food was just one part of the experience. This shift in perspective was perhaps his most valuable strategy, as it led to a richer social life that complemented his dietary needs rather than complicating them.

Through thoughtful planning, clear communication, and a thoughtful approach, Jack managed to seamlessly integrate his nutritional goals into his social life. These experiences enriched his journey, making his diet a part of his lifestyle rather than a constant challenge. Jack's narrative offers practical insights and encouragement for anyone looking to navigate social situations while staying true to their health commitments. With the right mindset and strategies, dining socially on a low-Carb Composition, high-Protein Composition diet not only becomes manageable but truly enjoyable.

4. BREAKFASTS TO START YOUR DAY

Imagine waking up to a morning that starts with energy, flavor, and a promise to keep your fitness goals on track! The breakfast recipes in this chapter are designed to do just that, providing you with low-Carb Composition, high-Protein Composition dishes that are quick to prepare and delicious to devour. Whether you're someone who loves to greet the dawn with a meal or you find yourself rushing through those early hours, the recipes here will fit seamlessly into your routine, supporting your weight loss and muscle-building desires without compromising your time.

Breakfast, often called the most important meal of the day, holds the key to kick-starting our metabolism and fueling our morning activities. But when you're committed to a low-Carb Composition high-Protein Composition diet, traditional breakfast options like cereal or toast won't suffice. That's where this chapter comes into play, transforming your morning meals into a powerhouse of nutrition that aligns perfectly with your dietary goals.

You'll discover dishes that come together in a flash, from smoothies rich with Protein Compositions and vibrant berries that blend in minutes, to omelets stuffed with fresh, crisp vegetables and robust cheeses. Perhaps you're feeding a family and need something that appeals to all. In that case, there are quick, skillet recipes that serve everyone at the table, supplying energy without the excess Carb Compositions.

For those leisurely weekend mornings, we haven't forgotten the joy of savoring a meal that feels like a treat. Indulge in pancakes, where almond and coconut flours take the stage, offering the fluffy texture and heartiness without the Carb Composition load. Pair them with a side of turkey bacon or a homemade sausage patty to keep your Protein Composition levels optimized.

Let each recipe in this chapter serve not just as a meal, but as an inspiration to maintain and thrive on your low-Carb Composition, high-Protein Composition journey. It's about making every meal an opportunity to nurture your body, cherish your health, and enjoy every bite along the way.

ZUCCHINI & FETA FRITTATA

PREP.TIME: 8 min.

COOK.TIME: 15 min.

METHOD OF COOK.: Baking

SERVES: 4

INGR: 4 large eggs

- 2 medium zucchini, grated

- ½ C. crumbled feta cheese

- 2 Tbls chopped fresh dill

- 1 Tbls olive oil

- Salt and pepper to taste

PROC: Preheat oven to 375°F (190°C)

- Whisk eggs in a bowl

- Squeeze excess moisture from zucchini, add to eggs along with feta, dill, salt, and pepper

- Heat olive oil in an oven-safe skillet over medium heat, pour egg mixture into skillet, cook until edges begin to set, about 3 min.

- Transfer skillet to oven, bake until set, 12 min.

TIPS: Serve with a side of mixed greens for extra fiber

- Can be stored in the refrigerator for up to 3 days

N.V.: Caloric Content: 220, Fat Composition: 18g, Carb Compositions: 3g, Protein Composition: 14g, Total Sugar: 2g

SMOKED SALMON SCRAMBLE

PREP.TIME: 5 min.

COOK.TIME: 10 min.

METHOD OF COOK.: Sauteing

SERVES: 2

INGR: 4 large eggs

- 100g smoked salmon, chopped

- 1 Tbls capers

- 2 Tbls cream cheese

- 1 Tbls chives, chopped

- Salt and black pepper to taste

PROC: Whisk eggs in a bowl

- Heat a non-stick skillet over medium heat, pour in eggs, gently scramble

- When eggs begin to set, add smoked salmon, cream cheese, capers, and chives, continue cooking until eggs are fully set

- Season with salt and pepper

TIPS: Garnish with additional chives for enhanced flavor

- Pairs well with a crisp, dry white wine

N.V.: Caloric Content: 320, Fat Composition: 22g, Carb Compositions: 3g, Protein Composition: 24g, Total Sugar: 2g

ALMOND BUTTER PANCAKES

PREP.TIME: 10 min.

COOK.TIME: 15 min.

METHOD OF COOK.: Griddling

SERVES: 3

INGR: 1 C. almond flour

- 2 large eggs

- ¼ C. almond butter

- ½ C. unsweetened almond milk

- 1 tsp vanilla extract

- 1 tsp baking powder

- Erythritol to taste

PROC: Mix almond flour, baking powder, erythritol in a bowl

- In another bowl, mix eggs, almond butter, almond milk, vanilla extract until smooth

- Combine wet and dry ingredients

- Heat a griddle over medium heat, drop batter to form pancakes, cook until bubbles form on top, flip and cook other side

TIPS: Top with a dollop of Greek yogurt

- Sweeten with a drizzle of monk fruit syrup

N.V.: Caloric Content: 265, Fat Composition: 20g, Carb Compositions: 10g, Protein Composition: 15g, Total Sugar: 1g

CAULIFLOWER HASH BROWNS

PREP.TIME: 12 min.

COOK.TIME: 18 min.

METHOD OF COOK.: Pan-frying

SERVES: 4

INGR: 1 medium cauliflower, grated

- 2 large eggs

- ¼ C. almond flour

- 2 Tbls chives, chopped

- Salt and pepper to taste

- 2 Tbls coconut oil

PROC: Mix grated cauliflower, eggs, almond flour, chives, salt, and pepper in a bowl

- Heat coconut oil in a skillet over medium heat

- Shape mixture into patties, fry until golden brown on both sides

TIPS: Serve hot with a side of Total Sugar-free ketchup

- Can be made in batches and frozen for later use

N.V.: Caloric Content: 140, Fat Composition: 9g, Carb Compositions: 8g, Protein Composition: 7g, Total Sugar: 3g

GREEK YOGURT PARFAIT

PREP.TIME: 5 min.

COOK.TIME: 0 min.

METHOD OF COOK.: Layering

SERVES: 1

INGR: ½ C. Greek yogurt, unsweetened

- ¼ C. raspberries

- 2 Tbls flaxseeds

- 1 Tbl coconut flakes

- Erythritol to taste

PROC: Layer Greek yogurt, raspberries, flaxseeds, and coconut flakes in a serving glass

- Sweeten with erythritol as desired

TIPS: Experiment with different berries for variety in flavor and color

- Can be prepared the night before for a quick breakfast

N.V.: Caloric Content: 180, Fat Composition: 9g, Carb Compositions: 12g, Protein Composition: 19g, Total Sugar: 4g

AVOCADO & EGG BREAKFAST BOWL

PREP.TIME: 7 min.

COOK.TIME: 3 min.

METHOD OF COOK.: Boiling

SERVES: 2

INGR: 1 large avocado, halved and pitted

- 2 eggs

- 1 cup spinach, fresh

- 1 Tbl olive oil

- Salt and pepper to taste

- Chili flakes (optional)

PROC: Boil eggs to desired doneness, peel

- In a bowl, arrange fresh spinach, place avocado halves on top, scoop out a bit of avocado to fit the eggs, place eggs in avocado halves

- Drizzle with olive oil, season with salt, pepper, and chili flakes

TIPS: Perfect with a cup of black coffee

- Sprinkle with hemp seeds for extra texture and nutrients

N.V.: Caloric Content: 300, Fat Composition: 25g, Carb Compositions: 10g, Protein Composition: 12g, Total Sugar: 2g

TURKEY AND SPINACH OMELETTE

PREP.TIME: 8 min.

COOK.TIME: 15 min.

METHOD OF COOK.: Whisking & Sauteing

SERVES: 1

INGR: 3 large eggs

- ½ C. cooked turkey breast, chopped

- ½ C. fresh spinach

- 1 Tbls grated Parmesan cheese

- 1 tsp olive oil

- Salt and pepper to taste

PROC: Whisk eggs with salt and pepper

- Heat olive oil in a skillet over medium heat, sauté spinach until wilted

- Add turkey, pour eggs over, cook until eggs are set, sprinkle with Parmesan, fold omelette

TIPS: Serve with a side of sautéed mushrooms for added flavor and nutrients

- Ideal for using up leftover turkey from meal preps

N.V.: Caloric Content: 290, Fat Composition: 17g, Carb Compositions: 2g, Protein Composition: 31g, Total Sugar: 1g

VANILLA CHAI PROTEIN COMPOSITION SHAKE

PREP.TIME: 5 min.

COOK.TIME: 0 min.

METHOD OF COOK.: Blending

SERVES: 1

INGR: 1 scoop vanilla Protein Composition powder

- 1 C. unsweetened almond milk

- ½ tsp ground cinnamon

- ¼ tsp ground ginger

- 1 pinch ground cloves

- 1 pinch ground cardamom

- 1 Tbls chia seeds

- 1 Tbls almond butter

- Ice cubes as needed

PROC: Combine Protein Composition powder, almond milk, cinnamon, ginger, cloves, cardamom, chia seeds, almond butter, and ice in a blender

- Blend until smooth

- Serve immediately

TIPS: Add a shot of espresso for a caffeine boost

- Use flax seeds instead of chia for a different texture

N.V.: Caloric Content: 280, Fat Composition: 15g, Carb Compositions: 9g, Protein Composition: 25g, Total Sugar: 1g

BERRY SILKEN TOFU SMOOTHIE

PREP.TIME: 6 min.

COOK.TIME: 0 min.

METHOD OF COOK.: Blending

SERVES: 2

INGR: ½ C. silken tofu

- 1 C. mixed berries (strawberries, blueberries, raspberries), frozen

- 1 C. spinach

- 2 Tbls flaxseed meal

- 1 C. unsweetened coconut water

- Stevia to taste

PROC: Add silken tofu, mixed berries, spinach, flaxseed meal, and coconut water to blender

- Blend until creamy and smooth

- Sweeten with stevia to taste

TIPS: Swap coconut water with almond milk for a creamier texture

- Add a scoop of nut butter for extra richness and Protein Composition

N.V.: Caloric Content: 150, Fat Composition: 4g, Carb Compositions: 14g, Protein Composition: 10g, Total Sugar: 6g

PUMPKIN PIE PROTEIN COMPOSITION SHAKE

PREP.TIME: 7 min.

COOK.TIME: 0 min.

METHOD OF COOK.: Blending

SERVES: 1

INGR: 1 scoop vanilla Protein Composition powder

- ¼ C. pumpkin puree, canned

- 1 tsp pumpkin pie spice

- 1 C. unsweetened almond milk

- 1 Tbls almond butter

- Ice cubes as needed

- Stevia to taste

PROC: Combine Protein Composition powder, pumpkin puree, pumpkin pie spice, almond milk, almond butter, ice, and stevia in a blender

- Blend until smooth

- Serve chilled

TIPS: Mix in a tsp of vanilla extract for enhanced flavor

- Top with a sprinkle of cinnamon for added spice

N.V.: Caloric Content: 265, Fat Composition: 14g, Carb Compositions: 12g, Protein Composition: 25g, Total Sugar: 3g

AVOCADO GREEN TEA SMOOTHIE

PREP.TIME: 8 min.

COOK.TIME: 0 min.

METHOD OF COOK.: Blending

SERVES: 1

INGR: ½ ripe avocado

- 1 scoop vanilla Protein Composition powder

- 1 C. spinach

- 1 C. brewed green tea, cooled

- 1 Tbls lemon juice

- Ice cubes as needed

PROC: Place avocado, Protein Composition powder, spinach, green tea, lemon juice, and ice in a blender

- Blend until very smooth

- Serve immediately

TIPS: Experiment with matcha powder instead of brewed green tea for an antioxidant boost

- Squeeze fresh lime juice for an extra tang

N.V.: Caloric Content: 290, Fat Composition: 17g, Carb Compositions: 12g, Protein Composition: 27g, Total Sugar: 1g

COCOA-ALMOND PROTEIN COMPOSITION SMOOTHIE

PREP.TIME: 5 min.

COOK.TIME: 0 min.

METHOD OF COOK.: Blending

SERVES: 1

INGR: 1 scoop chocolate Protein Composition powder

- 2 Tbls unsweetened cocoa powder

- 1 Tbls almond butter

- 1 C. unsweetened almond milk

- Ice cubes as needed

- Stevia to taste

PROC: Combine chocolate Protein Composition powder, cocoa powder, almond butter, almond milk, ice, and stevia in a blender

- Blend until creamy

- Serve chilled

TIPS: Add a pinch of sea salt to enhance the chocolate flavor

- Include a few mint leaves for a refreshing touch

N.V.: Caloric Content: 255, Fat Composition: 15g, Carb Compositions: 9g, Protein Composition: 24g, Total Sugar: 1g

TROPICAL TURMERIC PROTEIN COMPOSITION SMOOTHIE

PREP.TIME: 7 min.

COOK.TIME: 0 min.

METHOD OF COOK.: Blending

SERVES: 1

INGR: 1 scoop vanilla Protein Composition powder

- 1 C. coconut milk

- ½ C. pineapple chunks, frozen

- ½ tsp turmeric powder

- 1 Tbls flaxseed oil

- Ice cubes as needed

- Stevia to taste

PROC: Add Protein Composition powder, coconut milk, pineapple, turmeric, flaxseed oil, ice, and stevia to blender

- Blend until smooth and vibrant in color

- Serve immediately

TIPS: Substitute pineapple with mango for a different tropical taste

- Stir in a bit of ginger for extra zest and health benefits

N.V.: Caloric Content: 300, Fat Composition: 20g, Carb Compositions: 15g, Protein Composition: 22g, Total Sugar: 7g

MOCHA PROTEIN COMPOSITION FRAPPE

PREP.TIME: 6 min.

COOK.TIME: 0 min.

METHOD OF COOK.: Blending

SERVES: 1

INGR: 1 scoop chocolate Protein Composition powder

- 1 C. brewed coffee, cooled

- ½ C. unsweetened almond milk

- 1 Tbls unsweetened cocoa powder

- Ice cubes as needed

- Stevia to taste

PROC: Place Protein Composition powder, brewed coffee, almond milk, cocoa powder, ice, and stevia in a blender

- Blend until frothy and cold

- Serve in a tall glass

TIPS: Use decaf coffee if caffeine sensitivity is a concern

- Top with a light sprinkle of cinnamon for extra flavor

N.V.: Caloric Content: 160, Fat Composition: 3g, Carb Compositions: 8g, Protein Composition: 26g, Total Sugar: 0g

SAVORY TURKEY AND SPINACH FRITTATA

PREP.TIME: 15 min

COOK.TIME: 20 min

METHOD OF COOK.: Bake

SERVES: 6

INGR: 6 eggs

- ½ C. cottage cheese

- 1 C. spinach, chopped

- ½ C. turkey breast, cooked and diced

- ¼ C. feta cheese, crumbled

- 1 Tbls olive oil

- Salt and pepper to taste

PROC: Preheat oven to 375°F (190°C)

- Whisk eggs and cottage cheese together until smooth

- Stir in spinach, turkey, feta, and seasonings

- Heat olive oil in an oven-safe skillet over medium heat

- Pour egg mixture into skillet, cook for 3 min until edges begin to set

- Transfer skillet to oven, bake for 17 min until frittata is set

TIPS: Serve with a side of fresh arugula for added freshness

- Can be made ahead and refrigerated for a weekend brunch

N.V.: Caloric Content: 180, Fat Composition: 12g, Carb Compositions: 3g, Protein Composition: 15g, Total Sugar: 2g

CHIA AND BLUEBERRY PROTEIN COMPOSITION PANCAKES

PREP.TIME: 10 min

COOK.TIME: 15 min

METHOD OF COOK.: Pan Fry

SERVES: 4

INGR: ½ C. almond flour

- 2 Tbls coconut flour

- 1 Tbls chia seeds

- 2 eggs

- ½ C. Greek yogurt

- ¼ C. blueberries

- 1 tsp vanilla extract

- 1 tsp baking powder

- Stevia to taste

- Coconut oil for cooking

PROC: Mix almond flour, coconut flour, baking powder, and chia seeds in a bowl

- In another bowl, beat eggs, Greek yogurt, vanilla extract, and stevia together

- Combine wet and dry ingredients, fold in blueberries

- Heat a skillet with coconut oil over medium heat

- Scoop batter onto skillet, cook each side for about 2-3 min until golden and cooked through

TIPS: Top with a dollop of Greek yogurt and extra blueberries for serving

- Refrigerate leftover batter for up to 2 days

N.V.: Caloric Content: 190, Fat Composition: 14g, Carb Compositions: 8g, Protein Composition: 10g, Total Sugar: 3g

SMOKED SALMON AVOCADO BOATS

PREP.TIME: 5 min

COOK.TIME: 0 min

METHOD OF COOK.: No Cooking

SERVES: 2

INGR: 1 avocado, halved and pitted

- 4 oz. smoked salmon

- 2 Tbls Greek yogurt

- 1 Tbls chives, chopped

- Lemon zest and juice to taste

- Salt and pepper to taste

PROC: Scoop out some of the avocado flesh to create more space

- Mix Greek yogurt with lemon zest, juice, chives, salt, and pepper

- Fill avocado halves with smoked salmon and top with yogurt mixture

TIPS: Chill before serving to enhance the flavors

- Can be garnished with extra herbs or capers for an added zest

N.V.: Caloric Content: 300, Fat Composition: 22g, Carb Compositions: 9g, Protein Composition: 18g, Total Sugar: 2g

PEPPERONI AND EGG BREAKFAST PIZZA

PREP.TIME: 10 min

COOK.TIME: 15 min

METHOD OF COOK.: Bake

SERVES: 4

INGR: 4 eggs

- ¼ C. almond milk

- ½ C. mozzarella cheese, shredded

- ¼ C. pepperoni slices

- 1 Tbls coconut oil

- 1 low-Carb Composition tortilla wrap

- Salt and pepper to taste

PROC: Preheat oven to 400°F (204°C)

- Beat eggs with almond milk, salt, and pepper

- Heat coconut oil in a skillet, place tortilla wrap and pour egg mixture over it

- Sprinkle with mozzarella and pepperoni

- Place skillet in the oven, bake for 12-15 min until eggs are set and cheese is bubbly

TIPS: Serve immediately for a crispy crust

- Add a sprinkle of red pepper flakes for a spicy kick

N.V.: Caloric Content: 250, Fat Composition: 18g, Carb Compositions: 6g, Protein Composition: 15g, Total Sugar: 1g

COCONUT ALMOND PORRIDGE

PREP.TIME: 5 min

COOK.TIME: 10 min

METHOD OF COOK.: Simmer

SERVES: 2

INGR: ¼ C. coconut flour

- 2 Tbls ground flaxseed

- 1 C. almond milk

- 1 Tbls almond butter

- 1 Tbls shredded coconut

- Stevia to taste

- 1 tsp cinnamon

PROC: Combine coconut flour, flaxseed, almond milk, and cinnamon in a pot

- Bring to a simmer over medium heat, stir frequently to prevent clumping

- Once thickened, remove from heat, stir in almond butter and stevia

- Serve topped with shredded coconut

TIPS: Add a scoop of Protein Composition powder for an extra Protein Composition boost

- Use a variety of nuts and seeds for different textures and flavors

N.V.: Caloric Content: 215, Fat Composition: 14g, Carb Compositions: 12g, Protein Composition: 8g, Total Sugar: 1g

SAVORY CHORIZO EGG CUPS

PREP.TIME: 15 mins

COOK.TIME: 20 mins

METHOD OF COOK.: Oven Baking

SERVES: 6

INGR: 6 large eggs

- ½ C. cooked chorizo, crumbled

- ¼ C. diced bell peppers

- ¼ C. diced onions

- ¼ C. shredded cheddar cheese

- ¼ tsp smoked paprika

- ¼ tsp black pepper

- 1 Tbls chopped chives

PROC: Preheat oven to 375°F (190°C)

- Whisk eggs in a mixing bowl, then stir in chorizo, bell peppers, onions, cheese, smoked paprika, and black pepper until well mixed

- Grease a muffin tin and fill each cup with the mixture

- Bake for 18-20 minutes, or until eggs are set

- Let cool slightly before removing from muffin tin and sprinkle with chopped chives

TIPS: These cups can be made ahead and refrigerated for up to 3 days - Perfect for a Protein Composition-packed grab-and-go breakfast

N.V.: Caloric Content: 170, Fat Composition: 13g, Carb Compositions: 2g, Protein Composition: 11g, Total Sugar: 1g

5. LUNCHES FOR ENERGY AND FOCUS

Amidst a day brimming with tasks and responsibilities, lunch often becomes a hurried affair - a quick bite grabbed on the go or a non-descript meal eaten at the desk. Yet, this middle meal is crucial, and how you harness its potential can dramatically impact your energy levels and cognitive focus throughout the afternoon. The recipes in this chapter are not only designed to weave seamlessly into your busy schedule, but they also carry the promise of sustained energy and sharpened focus, turning a daily challenge into a delightful reprieve.

Imagine sitting down to a plate that doesn't just satisfy your hunger but also invigorates your body and mind for the hours to come. Each creation is a fusion of high-Protein Composition goodness, intertwined with low-Carb Composition attributes, perfectly engineered to keep that midday slump at bay. From vibrant, crisp salads dotted with Protein Composition-rich seeds and lean meats to warming soups that soothe the soul without weighing down the spirit, these meals are your weekday warriors.

Moreover, the joy of these recipes lies not just in their nutritional content but in their simplicity and speed. Envision preparing a delicious chicken avocado wrap in the time it takes your computer to reboot or assembling a smoked turkey and spinach salad while you clear your morning emails. These aren't just meals; they're your partners in the pursuit of a healthier, more energetic you.

So, let's transform your lunchtime into an opportunity—a moment to reset, recharge, and revitalize. With each recipe, you're not only nourishing your body but also fortifying your day against the inevitable challenges. Embrace these lunches as a tool to maintain your focus, boost your productivity, and edge you closer to your wellness goals, one satisfying bite at a time.

SMOKED SALMON AVOCADO SALAD

PREP.TIME: 15 min

COOK.TIME: 0 min

METHOD OF COOK.: No Cooking

SERVES: 2

INGR: 2 C. arugula

- 6 oz. smoked salmon, sliced

- 1 ripe avocado, cubed

- ¼ red onion, thinly sliced

- 2 Tbls capers

- 1 Tbls olive oil

- 2 tsp lemon juice

- Salt and pepper to taste

PROC: Combine arugula, smoked salmon, avocado, red onion, and capers in a large bowl

- In a small bowl, whisk together olive oil, lemon juice, salt, and pepper

- Pour the dressing over the salad and toss gently to coat

TIPS: Use wild-caught salmon for better flavor and nutrition

- Opt for freshly squeezed lemon juice for enhanced zestiness

N.V.: Caloric Content: 400, Fat Composition: 30g, Carb Compositions: 9g, Protein Composition: 24g, Total Sugar: 2g

CHICKEN CAESAR ESPUMA

PREP.TIME: 20 min

COOK.TIME: 0 min

METHOD OF COOK.: No Cooking

SERVES: 4

INGR: 1 lb. grilled chicken breast, chopped

- 1 large romaine lettuce, chopped

- ½ C. Parmesan cheese, grated

- ½ C. Greek yogurt

- 2 tsp Dijon mustard

- 1 garlic clove, minced

- 1 Tbls lemon juice

- 2 Tbls olive oil

- Anchovy paste to taste

- Salt and black pepper to taste

PROC: Combine lettuce, chicken, and Parmesan in a large salad bowl

- Blend Greek yogurt, Dijon mustard, minced garlic, lemon juice, olive oil, anchovy paste, salt, and black pepper to create the dressing

- Drizzle dressing over the salad and toss until evenly coated

TIPS: Opt for low-Fat Composition Greek yogurt to maintain the richness while cutting down on Fat Compositions

- Add a sprinkle of ground flaxseeds for an omega-3 boost

N.V.: Caloric Content: 345, Fat Composition: 19g, Carb Compositions: 4g, Protein Composition: 38g, Total Sugar: 2g

TOFU AND EDAMAME SALAD BOWL

PREP.TIME: 10 min

COOK.TIME: 0 min

METHOD OF COOK.: No Cooking

SERVES: 3

INGR: 8 oz. firm tofu, cubed

- 1 C. edamame, shelled

- 2 C. kale, chopped

- 1 red bell pepper, sliced

- 1 carrot, julienned

- 1 Tbls sesame oil

- 1 Tbls soy sauce

- 1 tsp wasabi paste

- 1 Tbls rice vinegar

- Sesame seeds for garnish

PROC: Mix tofu, edamame, kale, red bell pepper, and carrot in a large bowl

- In a small bowl, whisk together sesame oil, soy sauce, wasabi paste, and rice vinegar to make the dressing

- Toss the salad with the dressing and garnish with sesame seeds

TIPS: Press tofu before chopping to remove excess water and improve texture

- Wasabi paste can be adjusted for heat preference

N.V.: Caloric Content: 330, Fat Composition: 18g, Carb Compositions: 13g, Protein Composition: 29g, Total Sugar: 5g

BUFFALO CHICKEN SALAD

PREP.TIME: 15 min

COOK.TIME: 0 min

METHOD OF COOK.: No Cooking

SERVES: 2

INGR: 2 C. mixed greens

- 1 C. cooked chicken breast, shredded

- ¼ C. celery, thinly sliced

- ¼ C. carrot, shredded

- 2 Tbls blue cheese, crumbled

- 2 Tbls Greek yogurt

- 1 Tbls buffalo sauce

- 1 tsp apple cider vinegar

- Salt and pepper to taste

PROC: Mix greens, chicken, celery, carrot, and blue cheese in a bowl

- Combine Greek yogurt, buffalo sauce, apple cider vinegar, salt, and pepper to make the dressing

- Dress the salad and toss thoroughly to combine

TIPS: Choose a mild buffalo sauce or adjust the quantity to control spiciness

- Greek yogurt can be swapped with avocado for a creamier texture

N.V.: Caloric Content: 290, Fat Composition: 15g, Carb Compositions: 6g, Protein Composition: 30g, Total Sugar: 3g

MEDITERRANEAN TUNA & OLIVE SALAD

PREP.TIME: 10 mins

COOK.TIME: 0 mins

METHOD OF COOK.: No Cooking

SERVES: 4

INGR: 2 C. arugula, washed and dried

- 1 C. cherry tomatoes, halved

- 1 small cucumber, diced

- ¼ C. Kalamata olives, pitted and sliced

- 1 can tuna in olive oil, drained and flaked

- ¼ C. feta cheese, crumbled

- 2 Tbls extra-virgin olive oil

- 1 Tbls lemon juice

- ½ tsp dried oregano

- Salt and pepper to taste

PROC: In a large bowl, combine arugula, cherry tomatoes, cucumber, olives, tuna, and feta cheese

- Drizzle with olive oil and lemon juice, then sprinkle with oregano, salt, and pepper

- Toss gently to mix all ingredients without breaking the tuna flakes

TIPS: Add a handful of pumpkin seeds for extra crunch - Use mixed greens if you prefer a milder taste than arugula

N.V.: Caloric Content: 250, Fat Composition: 18g, Carb Compositions: 5g, Protein Composition: 20g, Total Sugar: 2g

STEAK AND ARUGULA SALAD

PREP.TIME: 15 min
COOK.TIME: 10 min
METHOD OF COOK.: Grilling
SERVES: 2
INGR: 12 oz. flank steak

- 3 C. arugula

- 1 C. cherry tomatoes, halved

- ½ red onion, thinly sliced

- 2 Tbls balsamic glaze

- 1 Tbls olive oil

- Salt and pepper to taste

PROC: Grill flank steak over medium-high heat until desired doneness, let rest for 5 min and slice thinly

- Combine arugula, cherry tomatoes, and red onion in a bowl

- Drizzle with balsamic glaze and olive oil

- Top with slices of steak and season with salt and pepper

TIPS: Opt for grass-fed steak for higher omega-3 content

- Letting the steak rest before slicing keeps it juicy and flavorful

N.V.: Caloric Content: 460, Fat Composition: 28g, Carb Compositions: 9g, Protein Composition: 44g, Total Sugar: 5g

MEDITERRANEAN CHICKPEA SALAD

PREP.TIME: 10 min
COOK.TIME: 0 min
METHOD OF COOK.: No Cooking
SERVES: 4
INGR: 2 C. chickpeas, drained and rinsed

- 1 C. cucumbers, diced

- 1 C. tomatoes, diced

- ½ C. red onion, finely chopped

- ½ C. Kalamata olives, halved

- ¼ C. feta cheese, crumbled

- 3 Tbls olive oil

- 2 Tbls lemon juice

- 1 tsp dried oregano

- Salt and pepper to taste

PROC: Mix chickpeas, cucumbers, tomatoes, red onion, Kalamata olives, and feta cheese in a large bowl

- In a separate bowl, whisk together olive oil, lemon juice, dried oregano, salt, and pepper to create dressing

- Pour dressing over the salad and toss well to combine

TIPS: Add chopped fresh parsley for enhanced flavor and freshness

- Substitute lemon juice with red wine vinegar for a different acidic twist

N.V.: Caloric Content: 345, Fat Composition: 20g, Carb Compositions: 29g, Protein Composition: 10g, Total Sugar: 5g

CREAMY COCONUT CHICKEN SOUP

PREP.TIME: 10 mins

COOK.TIME: 20 mins

METHOD OF COOK.: Stovetop

SERVES: 4

INGR: 1 Tbls coconut oil

- 1 lb. chicken breast, diced

- 1 C. coconut milk

- 3 C. chicken broth

- 1 C. spinach leaves

- 1 small zucchini, diced

- 1 red bell pepper, sliced

- 1 Tbls red curry paste

- 1 Tbls ginger, minced

- Salt and pepper to taste

PROC: In a large pot, heat coconut oil over medium heat and cook the chicken until golden

- Add red curry paste and ginger, stirring until fragrant

- Pour in coconut milk and chicken broth, bringing to a simmer

- Add zucchini, bell pepper, and spinach; cook for 10-12 minutes until vegetables are tender

- Season with salt and pepper before serving

TIPS: Add a squeeze of lime for extra flavor

- Garnish with fresh cilantro for a burst of freshness

N.V.: Caloric Content: 280, Fat Composition: 18g, Carb Compositions: 6g, Protein Composition: 24g, Total Sugar: 2g

SPICY SHRIMP & TOMATO BISQUE

PREP.TIME: 10 mins

COOK.TIME: 20 mins

METHOD OF COOK.: Stovetop

SERVES: 4

INGR: 1 Tbls olive oil

- 1 lb. shrimp, peeled and deveined

- 1 small onion, diced

- 2 C. diced tomatoes

- 3 C. vegetable broth

- 1 Tbls tomato paste

- 1 Tbls hot sauce

- 1 tsp smoked paprika

- Salt and pepper to taste

PROC: In a large pot, heat olive oil over medium heat and cook shrimp until pink, then set aside

- In the same pot, add onion, cooking until softened

- Stir in tomatoes, tomato paste, hot sauce, and paprika, cooking for 5 minutes

- Add vegetable broth, bring to a simmer for 10 minutes

- Return shrimp to pot and season with salt and pepper

TIPS: Serve with a side of avocado slices for added healthy Fat Compositions - Adjust the hot sauce to your preferred spice level

N.V.: Caloric Content: 220, Fat Composition: 8g, Carb Compositions: 10g, Protein Composition: 28g, Total Sugar: 4g

CHICKEN ZOODLE SOUP

PREP.TIME: 10 min

COOK.TIME: 20 min

METHOD OF COOK.: Stovetop

SERVES: 4

INGR: 2 C. cooked chicken breast, shredded

- 4 medium zucchinis, spiralized

- 1 Tbls avocado oil

- 1 qt. chicken stock

- 1 tsp garlic powder

- 1 medium onion, chopped

- 1 C. celery, chopped

- Salt and black pepper to taste

- Lemon wedges for serving

PROC: Heat avocado oil in a large saucepan over medium heat

- Sauté onion and celery until tender

- Add chicken stock, garlic powder, salt, and pepper and bring to a low boil

- Add chicken and zoodles and simmer for 10 minutes

- Serve with a squeeze of lemon

TIPS: Add fresh herbs like dill or parsley for enhanced flavor

- Squeeze lemon just before serving to maintain fresh zestiness

N.V.: Caloric Content: 150, Fat Composition: 4g, Carb Compositions: 8g, Protein Composition: 22g, Total Sugar: 5g

BROCCOLI & CHEDDAR SOUP

PREP.TIME: 10 mins

COOK.TIME: 20 mins

METHOD OF COOK.: Stovetop

SERVES: 4

INGR: 1 Tbls butter

- 1 small onion, diced

- 2 C. broccoli florets

- 3 C. chicken broth

- 1 C. shredded cheddar cheese

- 1 C. unsweetened almond milk

- ¼ tsp ground nutmeg

- Salt and pepper to taste

PROC: In a large pot, melt butter over medium heat and sauté onion until soft

- Add broccoli and chicken broth, simmering for 15 minutes until broccoli is tender

- Use an immersion blender to puree the soup to your desired texture

- Stir in cheddar cheese, almond milk, and nutmeg until cheese is melted

- Season with salt and pepper before serving

TIPS: Sprinkle with extra cheddar on top for a cheesier flavor - Add a pinch of cayenne for a subtle kick

N.V.: Caloric Content: 240, Fat Composition: 18g, Carb Compositions: 6g, Protein Composition: 15g, Total Sugar: 1g

ZUCCHINI BASIL SOUP

PREP.TIME: 10 mins

COOK.TIME: 20 mins

METHOD OF COOK.: Stovetop

SERVES: 4

INGR: 1 Tbls olive oil

- 1 small onion, diced

- 2 cloves garlic, minced

- 3 C. zucchini, sliced

- 3 C. vegetable broth

- ½ C. fresh basil leaves

- 1 C. coconut milk

- Salt and pepper to taste

PROC: In a large pot, heat olive oil over medium heat and sauté onion and garlic until fragrant

- Add zucchini and vegetable broth, bring to a simmer and cook for 15 minutes until zucchini is tender

- Blend with an immersion blender until smooth

- Stir in basil leaves and coconut milk, season with salt and pepper, and serve warm

TIPS: Garnish with fresh basil and a sprinkle of pumpkin seeds for crunch - Add a squeeze of lemon juice for extra brightness

N.V.: Caloric Content: 180, Fat Composition: 14g, Carb Compositions: 8g, Protein Composition: 4g, Total Sugar: 3g

SPICY TOMATO & TUNA STEW

PREP.TIME: 10 min

COOK.TIME: 20 min

METHOD OF COOK.: Stovetop

SERVES: 4

INGR: 2 cans tuna in olive oil, drained

- 1 Tbls coconut oil

- 1 onion, chopped

- 2 garlic cloves, minced

- 1 jalapeño, seeded and diced

- 1 can (14 oz.) diced tomatoes

- 4 C. chicken broth

- 1 tsp chili powder

- Salt to taste

- Chopped cilantro for garnish

PROC: Heat coconut oil in a pot over medium heat

- Add onion, garlic, and jalapeño, cook until onion is translucent

- Stir in diced tomatoes and chili powder, cook for another minute

- Add tuna and chicken broth, bring to a boil then simmer for 15 minutes

- Season with salt

- Garnish with cilantro before serving

TIPS: Include a splash of lime juice for a refreshing touch

- Serve with a slice of low-Carb Composition, high-fiber bread

N.V.: Caloric Content: 190, Fat Composition: 6g, Carb Compositions: 9g, Protein Composition: 24g, Total Sugar: 5g

SPICED CAULIFLOWER & ALMOND SOUP

PREP.TIME: 10 mins

COOK.TIME: 20 mins

METHOD OF COOK.: Stovetop

SERVES: 4

INGR: 1 Tbls coconut oil

- 1 small onion, diced

- 2 C. cauliflower florets

- ½ C. slivered almonds

- 4 C. vegetable broth

- 1 tsp ground cumin

- 1 tsp ground coriander

- Salt and pepper to taste

PROC: In a pot, heat coconut oil over medium heat and sauté onion until soft

- Add cauliflower, almonds, cumin, and coriander, stirring to coat

- Pour in vegetable broth and bring to a simmer, cooking for 15 minutes until cauliflower is tender

- Blend until smooth and season with salt and pepper to taste

TIPS: Top with a few toasted almonds and a drizzle of olive oil for extra flavor - A pinch of smoked paprika adds a nice depth

N.V.: Caloric Content: 210, Fat Composition: 16g, Carb Compositions: 10g, Protein Composition: 6g, Total Sugar: 2g

ZESTY CHICKEN CAESAR WRAP

PREP.TIME: 10 min.

COOK.TIME: 0 min.

METHOD OF COOK.: No Cooking

SERVES: 2

INGR: 2 whole grain low-Carb Composition wraps

- 1 C. cooked chicken breast, thinly sliced

- ¼ C. Parmesan cheese, shaved

- 1 C. romaine lettuce, chopped

- 2 Tbls Caesar dressing, Total Sugar-free

- 1 tsp lemon juice

- 1 tsp black pepper

PROC: Spread Caesar dressing evenly on each wrap

- Layer chicken slices, romaine lettuce, and Parmesan cheese on top

- Drizzle with lemon juice and sprinkle black pepper

- Roll tightly and cut in half

TIPS: Try adding anchovies for a flavor boost

- Opt for a whole grain or low-Carb Composition wrap to maintain nutritional goals

N.V.: Caloric Content: 320, Fat Composition: 18g, Carb Compositions: 12g, Protein Composition: 25g, Total Sugar: 2g

SPICY TOFU WRAP WITH AVOCADO

PREP.TIME: 15 min.

COOK.TIME: 5 min.

METHOD OF COOK.: Pan-Searing

SERVES: 1

INGR: 1 small low-Carb Composition tortilla

- ½ C. firm tofu, diced

- ½ avocado, sliced

- 1 Tbls coconut oil

- 1 Tbls soy sauce, low sodium

- 1 tsp sriracha

- ¼ C. red cabbage, shredded

- 1 Tbls cilantro, chopped

PROC: Pan-sear tofu in coconut oil until golden

- Toss tofu with soy sauce and sriracha

- Lay tofu, avocado slices, red cabbage, and cilantro on tortilla

- Roll tightly and slice in half

TIPS: Incorporate other vegetables like carrots or bell peppers for extra nutrients

- For extra spice, increase sriracha amount

N.V.: Caloric Content: 295, Fat Composition: 21g, Carb Compositions: 15g, Protein Composition: 12g, Total Sugar: 2g

TURKEY RANCH CLUB

PREP.TIME: 10 min.

COOK.TIME: 0 min.

METHOD OF COOK.: No Cooking

SERVES: 2

INGR: 2 large lettuce leaves

- 4 oz. turkey breast, sliced

- 2 slices tomato

- 2 strips turkey bacon, cooked and crisp

- 1 Tbls ranch dressing, Total Sugar-free

- 1 Tbls avocado, mashed

- 1 tsp dried dill

PROC: Lay lettuce leaves flat

- Spread each leaf with mashed avocado and ranch dressing

- Add turkey slices, turkey bacon, and tomato

- Sprinkle dill on top

- Roll lettuce tightly around fillings

TIPS: Swap turkey with chicken for a different Protein Composition option

- Add cucumber strips for extra crunch

N.V.: Caloric Content: 240, Fat Composition: 13g, Carb Compositions: 8g, Protein Composition: 25g, Total Sugar: 3g

SALMON AND CREAM CHEESE BAGEL

PREP.TIME: 15 min.

COOK.TIME: 0 min.

METHOD OF COOK.: No Cooking

SERVES: 1

INGR: 1 low-Carb Composition bagel, halved and toasted

- 2 oz. smoked salmon

- 1 Tbls cream cheese, low-Fat Composition

- 2 tsp capers

- 1 Tbls red onion, thinly sliced

- 1 tsp fresh dill

PROC: Spread cream cheese on both halves of toasted bagel

- Layer smoked salmon, capers, and red onion on one half

- Sprinkle with dill

- Top with the other bagel half

TIPS: Consider using a flavored low-Fat Composition cream cheese to enhance taste

- Adding cucumber slices can introduce a refreshing crunch

N.V.: Caloric Content: 310, Fat Composition: 15g, Carb Compositions: 23g, Protein Composition: 22g, Total Sugar: 4g

BEEF AND HORSERADISH CREAM WRAP

PREP.TIME: 15 min.

COOK.TIME: 0 min.

METHOD OF COOK.: No Cooking

SERVES: 2

INGR: 2 flaxseed wraps

- ½ lb. roast beef, thinly sliced

- 2 Tbls horseradish cream sauce

- ¼ C. arugula

- 2 Tbls red bell pepper, julienned

- 1 tsp olive oil

- salt and pepper to taste

PROC: Lay out wraps

- Spread horseradish cream sauce evenly on each

- Layer roast beef, arugula, and bell pepper

- Drizzle olive oil and season with salt and pepper

- Roll wraps tightly and slice in half

TIPS: Option to add sliced pickles for tanginess

- Use extra horseradish for a stronger kick

N.V.: Caloric Content: 350, Fat Composition: 20g, Carb Compositions: 18g, Protein Composition: 26g, Total Sugar: 2g

EGG SALAD LETTUCE WRAP

PREP.TIME: 10 min.

COOK.TIME: 0 min.

METHOD OF COOK.: No Cooking

SERVES: 2

INGR: 4 large eggs, hard-boiled and chopped

- 2 Tbls mayonnaise, low-Fat Composition

- 1 tsp mustard

- 1 Tbls chives, chopped

- 4 leaves of iceberg lettuce

- 1 tsp paprika

- salt and pepper to taste

PROC: Mix eggs with mayonnaise, mustard, chives, paprika, salt, and pepper

- Spoon egg mixture into the center of each lettuce leaf

- Fold the sides of the lettuce over the filling, securing with a toothpick

TIPS: Use Greek yogurt instead of mayonnaise for a healthier alternative

- Add diced celery for crunch and freshness

N.V.: Caloric Content: 180, Fat Composition: 12g, Carb Compositions: 4g, Protein Composition: 12g, Total Sugar: 2g

6. HIGH-PROTEIN COMPOSITION SNACKS

In the bustling rhythm of our daily lives, finding the time to prepare healthy meals can feel like a Herculean task. Snacks, often grabbed on the go, end up being overlooked as a vital part of our diet strategy. Yet, it's precisely in these bite-sized eats where a golden opportunity lies, especially for those of us committed to a low-Carb Composition, high-Protein Composition regimen. High-Protein Composition snacks aren't just a filler to curb hunger—they are stepping stones towards achieving your wellness goals, be it shedding pounds, sculpting muscle, or boosting energy.

Imagine this: It's mid-afternoon; lunch seems like a distant memory and dinner is on the distant horizon. Your stomach starts rumbling. Without a plan, you might reach for whatever is closest, often resulting in choices high in Carb Compositions and Total Sugars, which spike your insulin levels and crash your energy. Instead, consider the quick and mindful fix of a Protein Composition-packed snack that keeps the metabolism firing and cravings at bay.

What makes these snacks different? They are crafted not only to satisfy hunger but to provide sustained energy, build muscle, and help in recovery post-exercise. Consider a creamy Greek yogurt with a sprinkle of chia seeds, a hard-boiled egg seasoned with a pinch of Himalayan salt, or a handful of almonds. These aren't merely snacks; they are miniature nutritional powerhouses that keep your body in peak performance mode.

Furthermore, high-Protein Composition snacks can be incredibly versatile and, dare I say, delicious. They break the monotony of everyday meals and open up new avenues for culinary creativity without the guilt.

Whether you're a busy professional, a multitasking parent, or someone navigating the complexities of dieting, these snacks ensure you stay on track with your health goals without compromising on taste.

In the upcoming pages, you'll uncover recipes that not only align with your dietary needs but are also quick to prepare. From savory delights to sweet indulgences, each recipe is designed to be straightforward yet flavorful, proving that healthy eating doesn't have to be bland or burdensome. Dive into these snack ideas with enthusiasm, knowing each bite is crafted to support not just your physical health but also your bustling lifestyle.

TURKEY & SPINACH PINWHEELS

PREP.TIME: 15 min

COOK.TIME: 0 min

METHOD OF COOK.: No Cooking

SERVES: 10

INGR: 4 large whole wheat tortillas

- 8 oz. deli turkey slices

- 1 C. fresh spinach

- 1/2 C. cream cheese, softened

- 1/4 C. red bell pepper, finely chopped

- 1/4 C. shredded cheddar cheese

- 1 Tbls Dijon mustard

PROC: Spread cream cheese evenly on tortillas

- Layer turkey slices on top followed by spinach, bell peppers, and cheddar

- Drizzle Dijon mustard over the ingredients

- Tightly roll up the tortillas

- Slice into 1-inch thick pinwheels

TIPS: Chill in the refrigerator for a firmer texture before slicing

- Can be made ahead and stored in an airtight container for up to two days

N.V.: Caloric Content: 180, Fat Composition: 9g, Carb Compositions: 9g, Protein Composition: 16g, Total Sugar: 2g

CHIA SEED & COCONUT ENERGY BITES

PREP.TIME: 10 min

COOK.TIME: 0 min

METHOD OF COOK.: No Cooking

SERVES: 15

INGR: 1/2 C. chia seeds

- 1/2 C. flax seeds

- 1/2 C. desiccated coconut

- 1/4 C. unsweetened Protein Composition powder

- 1/4 C. almond butter

- 3 Tbls coconut oil, melted

- 2 Tbls monk fruit sweetener

PROC: Mix all ingredients in a bowl until well combined

- Form the mixture into small, bite-sized balls

- Place in the refrigerator to set

TIPS: Roll in extra desiccated coconut for added texture

- Keep refrigerated for best freshness

N.V.: Caloric Content: 140, Fat Composition: 10g, Carb Compositions: 5g, Protein Composition: 7g, Total Sugar: 0g

SAVORY ALMOND & ROSEMARY BARS

PREP.TIME: 20 min

COOK.TIME: 0 min

METHOD OF COOK.: No Cooking

SERVES: 8

INGR: 1 C. almonds, finely chopped

- 1/2 C. sunflower seeds

- 1/4 C. pumpkin seeds

- 2 Tbls ground flaxseed

- 2 Tbls fresh rosemary, finely chopped

- 1/3 C. parmesan cheese, grated

- 1/4 C. olive oil

- Salt and pepper to taste

PROC: Combine all ingredients in a large bowl

- Press the mixture firmly into a lined baking dish

- Chill in the refrigerator until firm, then cut into bars

TIPS: Store in a cool, dry place for up to a week

- Infuse oil with rosemary overnight for enhanced flavor

N.V.: Caloric Content: 220, Fat Composition: 18g, Carb Compositions: 6g, Protein Composition: 8g, Total Sugar: 1g

HERBED YOGURT CHEESE BALLS

PREP.TIME: 15 min

COOK.TIME: 0 min

METHOD OF COOK.: No Cooking

SERVES: 12

INGR: 2 C. Greek yogurt, strained overnight

- 1 Tbls chives, chopped

- 1 Tbls parsley, chopped

- 1 tsp garlic powder

- Salt and pepper to taste

- 1/4 C. almonds, finely crushed

PROC: Mix yogurt with herbs, garlic powder, salt, and pepper

- Form into small balls

- Roll the balls in crushed almonds to coat

- Refrigerate until firm

TIPS: Use cheesecloth to strain yogurt for thicker cheese balls

- Flavor varies with different herbs

N.V.: Caloric Content: 80, Fat Composition: 5g, Carb Compositions: 3g, Protein Composition: 6g, Total Sugar: 2g

SMOKED SALMON CUCUMBER ROLLS

PREP.TIME: 10 min

COOK.TIME: 0 min

METHOD OF COOK.: No Cooking

SERVES: 8

INGR: 1 English cucumber, thinly sliced lengthwise

- 4 oz. smoked salmon, thinly sliced

- 1/4 C. cream cheese, softened

- 1 Tbls capers, drained

- 1 Tbls dill, chopped

- Lemon zest for garnish

PROC: Spread cream cheese on cucumber slices

- Top with slices of smoked salmon

- Add capers and dill, then roll up tightly

TIPS: Garnish with lemon zest for extra flavor

- Serve immediately or chill to enhance flavors

N.V.: Caloric Content: 70, Fat Composition: 4g, Carb Compositions: 2g, Protein Composition: 5g, Total Sugar: 1g

PISTACHIO & CRANBERRY PROTEIN COMPOSITION SQUARES

PREP.TIME: 15 min

COOK.TIME: 0 min

METHOD OF COOK.: No Cooking

SERVES: 10

INGR: 1 C. pistachios, crushed

- 1/2 C. dried cranberries

- 1/4 C. hemp seeds

- 1/3 C. honey

- 1/2 C. almond butter

- 1 tsp vanilla extract

PROC: Mix all ingredients in a bowl until well combined

- Press into a lined square pan

- Refrigerate until firm, then cut into squares

TIPS: Can be frozen for longer storage

- Use raw honey for better nutritional benefits

N.V.: Caloric Content: 200, Fat Composition: 12g, Carb Compositions: 18g, Protein Composition: 6g, Total Sugar: 11g

AVOCADO LIME MOUSSE

PREP.TIME: 10 min

COOK.TIME: 0 min

METHOD OF COOK.: No Cooking

SERVES: 4

INGR: 2 ripe avocados, peeled and pitted

- Juice of 2 limes

- 1/4 C. coconut cream

- 2 Tbls erythritol

- 1 tsp vanilla extract

PROC: Blend all ingredients in a blender until smooth

- Pour into small serving dishes

- Chill in the refrigerator before serving

TIPS: Top with a slice of lime or mint for extra flair

- Use ripe avocados for the best texture

N.V.: Caloric Content: 230, Fat Composition: 20g, Carb Compositions: 10g, Protein Composition: 3g, Total Sugar: 1g

SUNDRIED TOMATO & FETA HUMMUS

PREP.TIME: 15 min

COOK.TIME: 0 min

METHOD OF COOK.: No Cooking

SERVES: 4

INGR: 1 C. cannellini beans, drained

- ⅓ C. sundried tomatoes in oil, drained and chopped

- 2 Tbls feta cheese, crumbled

- 2 Tbls tahini

- 1 Tbls olive oil

- 1 clove garlic, minced

- Juice of 1 lemon

- Salt and pepper to taste

PROC: Combine all ingredients in a food processor

- Blend until smooth, scraping down the sides as needed

- If needed, add a few teaspoons of water to reach desired consistency

TIPS: Serve with a drizzle of olive oil and a sprinkle of paprika for a touch of spicy sweetness

- Can be stored in the refrigerator for up to 5 days

N.V.: Caloric Content: 180, Fat Composition: 10g, Carb Compositions: 15g, Protein Composition: 7g, Total Sugar: 2g

AVOCADO AND LIME CREMA

PREP.TIME: 10 min

COOK.TIME: 0 min

METHOD OF COOK.: No Cooking

SERVES: 6

INGR: 2 ripe avocados, peeled and pitted

- ½ C. Greek yogurt, plain

- Juice of 2 limes

- 1 Tbls cilantro, chopped

- 1 small jalapeño, seeded and minced

- Salt to taste

PROC: Place all ingredients in a blender

- Purée until smooth and creamy

- Adjust seasoning with additional lime juice or salt if necessary

TIPS: Store in an airtight container with a piece of plastic wrap pressed directly onto the surface of the crema to prevent browning

- Perfect as a topping for grilled chicken or fish

N.V.: Caloric Content: 120, Fat Composition: 9g, Carb Compositions: 8g, Protein Composition: 4g, Total Sugar: 1g

SMOKED SALMON PÂTÉ

PREP.TIME: 20 min

COOK.TIME: 0 min

METHOD OF COOK.: No Cooking

SERVES: 8

INGR: 8 oz. smoked salmon

- ⅓ C. cream cheese, softened

- 2 Tbls sour cream

- 1 Tbls fresh dill, chopped

- 1 tsp horseradish

- 1 Tbls lemon juice

- Black pepper to taste

PROC: Combine all ingredients in a food processor

- Pulse until well mixed but still slightly chunky, for texture

- Adjust the seasoning as per taste preference

TIPS: Great served on cucumber slices or low-Carb Composition toast

- Can experiment with adding capers for an extra zing

N.V.: Caloric Content: 100, Fat Composition: 7g, Carb Compositions: 2g, Protein Composition: 9g, Total Sugar: 1g

HERBED GOAT CHEESE SPREAD

PREP.TIME: 10 min

COOK.TIME: 0 min

METHOD OF COOK.: No Cooking

SERVES: 5

INGR: 6 oz. goat cheese

- 1 Tbls olive oil

- 2 tsp mixed herbs (such as thyme, oregano, and basil), finely chopped

- 1 clove garlic, minced

- Salt and pepper to taste

PROC: Stir all ingredients together until well combined

- Adjust herbs and seasoning to taste

- Let sit at room temperature for 10 minutes before serving to enhance flavors

TIPS: Ideal for spreading on flaxseed crackers or as a stuffing for mini bell peppers

- Can be made ahead and stored in the refrigerator for up to a week

N.V.: Caloric Content: 90, Fat Composition: 8g, Carb Compositions: 1g, Protein Composition: 5g, Total Sugar: 0g

ALMOND BUTTER AND CHIA SEED SPREAD

PREP.TIME: 15 min

COOK.TIME: 0 min

METHOD OF COOK.: No Cooking

SERVES: 10

INGR: ¾ C. almond butter

- 2 Tbls chia seeds

- 1 Tbls flaxseed meal

- 2 tsp cinnamon

- Stevia to taste

- Salt to taste

PROC: Mix almond butter with chia seeds, flaxseed meal, cinnamon, stevia, and salt until evenly distributed

- Let sit for 5 minutes to allow chia seeds to swell slightly

TIPS: This spread goes well on high Protein Composition pancakes or mixed into a smoothie for extra texture and flavor

- Keeps well in the refrigerator for up to a month

N.V.: Caloric Content: 160, Fat Composition: 14g, Carb Compositions: 6g, Protein Composition: 5g, Total Sugar: 1g

KICKED-UP COTTAGE CHEESE DIP

PREP.TIME: 10 min

COOK.TIME: 0 min

METHOD OF COOK.: No Cooking

SERVES: 4

INGR: 1 C. cottage cheese, full-Fat Composition

- 1 medium red bell pepper, finely diced

- 2 green onions, thinly sliced

- 1 Tbls hot sauce

- 1 tsp smoked paprika

- Salt and pepper to taste

PROC: Puree cottage cheese until smooth

- Stir in bell pepper, green onions, hot sauce, and smoked paprika

- Season with salt and pepper to taste

TIPS: Serve chilled with raw vegetables or low Carb Composition pita chips for dipping

- Adjust the amount of hot sauce to suit your taste for heat

N.V.: Caloric Content: 90, Fat Composition: 5g, Carb Compositions: 3g, Protein Composition: 9g, Total Sugar: 2g

BASIL PESTO RICOTTA DIP

PREP.TIME: 15 min

COOK.TIME: 0 min

METHOD OF COOK.: No Cooking

SERVES: 6

INGR: 1 C. ricotta cheese

- ¼ C. basil pesto

- 2 Tbls pine nuts, toasted

- 1 Tbls Parmesan cheese, grated

- Salt and pepper to taste

PROC: Combine ricotta and pesto in a bowl

- Mix until well blended

- Stir in pine nuts and Parmesan

- Season with salt and pepper according to your preference

TIPS: Can be served with vegetable sticks or used as a spread on low-Carb Composition wraps

- For a creamier texture, blend the ingredients together in a food processor

N.V.: Caloric Content: 120, Fat Composition: 9g, Carb Compositions: 4g, Protein Composition: 7g, Total Sugar: 1g

CHOCOLATE HAZELNUT PROTEIN COMPOSITION BITES

PREP.TIME: 10 mins

COOK.TIME: 0 mins

METHOD OF COOK.: No Cooking

SERVES: 12

INGR: 1 C. hazelnuts, finely chopped

- ½ C. chocolate Protein Composition powder

- ¼ C. almond butter

- 2 Tbls cocoa powder, unsweetened

- 1 Tbls coconut oil, melted

- 1 tsp vanilla extract

- Stevia or erythritol to taste

PROC: Combine all ingredients in a bowl until well mixed

- Roll mixture into small balls and chill in the refrigerator for 15 minutes before serving

- Store in an airtight container

TIPS: Roll bites in extra cocoa powder for a richer chocolate flavor - For extra crunch, add a tablespoon of chia seeds

N.V.: Caloric Content: 130, Fat Composition: 10g, Carb Compositions: 5g, Protein Composition: 7g, Total Sugar: 1g

LEMON CHIA SEED PROTEIN COMPOSITION BARS

PREP.TIME: 20 min.

COOK.TIME: 0 min.

METHOD OF COOK.: No Cooking

SERVES: 8

INGR: 1 C. rolled oats

- 1/2 C. chia seeds

- 1/2 C. Protein Composition powder, unflavored

- 1/4 C. shredded coconut

- 1/4 C. coconut oil, melted

- 1/4 C. lemon juice

- Zest of 1 lemon

- 1/4 C. almond butter

- 1/4 C. Erythritol

- 1 tsp vanilla extract

PROC: Mix rolled oats, chia seeds, Protein Composition powder, and shredded coconut in a bowl

- In another bowl, combine melted coconut oil, lemon juice, lemon zest, almond butter, Erythritol, and vanilla extract

- Mix wet and dry ingredients until well combined

- Press mixture into a lined square pan and refrigerate until set

TIPS: Cut into bars while cold for cleaner slices

- Store in the refrigerator for up to 1 week

N.V.: Caloric Content: 180, Fat Composition: 11g, Carb Compositions: 12g, Protein Composition: 10g, Total Sugar: 1g

RASPBERRY COCONUT PROTEIN COMPOSITION PUDDING

PREP.TIME: 10 min.

COOK.TIME: 0 min.

METHOD OF COOK.: Mixing

SERVES: 4

INGR: 1 C. raspberries

- 1 C. Greek yogurt, unsweetened

- 1/2 C. Protein Composition powder, vanilla-flavored

- 1/4 C. flaked coconut, unsweetened

- 2 Tbls chia seeds

- Erythritol to taste

PROC: Blend raspberries until smooth

- Mix Greek yogurt, vanilla Protein Composition powder, and Erythritol in a bowl

- Stir in blended raspberries, flaked coconut, and chia seeds until well combined

- Chill in the refrigerator until set

TIPS: Serve topped with additional raspberries and a sprinkle of coconut for texture

- The pudding thickens further if left overnight in the fridge

N.V.: Caloric Content: 190, Fat Composition: 7g, Carb Compositions: 12g, Protein Composition: 20g, Total Sugar: 4g

PEANUT BUTTER PROTEIN COMPOSITION TRUFFLES

PREP.TIME: 25 min.

COOK.TIME: 0 min.

METHOD OF COOK.: Mixing

SERVES: 10

INGR: 1 C. peanut butter, unsweetened

- 1/2 C. almond flour

- 1/3 C. Protein Composition powder, chocolate-flavored

- 1/4 C. flaxseed meal

- Erythritol to taste

- 1 tsp vanilla extract

PROC: Mix all ingredients in a large bowl until they form a dough-like consistency

- Roll mixture into small balls

- Chill in the refrigerator until firm

TIPS: Roll in cocoa powder or crushed nuts for an extra layer of flavor

- Keep refrigerated in an airtight container to maintain freshness

N.V.: Caloric Content: 160, Fat Composition: 10g, Carb Compositions: 8g, Protein Composition: 10g, Total Sugar: 2g

VANILLA COCONUT CHIA PUDDING

PREP.TIME: 5 mins

COOK.TIME: 0 mins

METHOD OF COOK.: No Cooking

SERVES: 4

INGR: 1 C. unsweetened almond milk

- ¼ C. chia seeds

- 1 scoop vanilla Protein Composition powder

- 1 Tbls shredded coconut, unsweetened

- ½ tsp vanilla extract

- Stevia to taste

PROC: In a bowl, whisk almond milk, chia seeds, Protein Composition powder, shredded coconut, and vanilla extract

- Pour mixture into serving glasses and refrigerate for at least 4 hours or overnight until thickened

- Stir before serving

TIPS: Top with fresh berries or a sprinkle of cinnamon for added flavor - This pudding keeps well in the fridge for up to 3 days

N.V.: Caloric Content: 160, Fat Composition: 8g, Carb Compositions: 8g, Protein Composition: 10g, Total Sugar: 1g

ALMOND JOY PROTEIN COMPOSITION SHAKE

PREP.TIME: 5 min.

COOK.TIME: 0 min.

METHOD OF COOK.: Blending

SERVES: 2

INGR: 1 C. almond milk, unsweetened

- 2 Tbls almond butter

- 2 Tbls unsweetened cocoa powder

- 1 scoop Protein Composition powder, chocolate-flavored

- 1 Tbls coconut flakes, unsweetened

- Stevia to taste

- Ice as needed

PROC: Blend all ingredients until smooth

TIPS: Add a few drops of coconut extract for enhanced flavor

- Use crushed ice for a thicker texture

- Serve immediately for best taste and consistency

N.V.: Caloric Content: 180, Fat Composition: 14g, Carb Compositions: 7g, Protein Composition: 12g, Total Sugar: 1g

7. DINNER DELIGHTS

As the sun dips below the horizon and dusk begins to blanket the sky, there's a universal call to the dinner table—a time to unwind, gather, and savor not only the food but the company of loved ones. In this chapter, "Dinner Delights," we embrace the joy of evening meals that fortify both body and soul without complicating your busy life.

Dinner is often the main meal that brings families together, and it holds a special place in our routines and rituals. Yet, striking the balance between nutritious, Protein Composition-rich, low-Carb Composition options and quick, appealing dishes can seem daunting. Imagine plates filled with robust flavors, textures that delight both young and old, and all aligning with your health goals—this is what we aim to create in your kitchen every night.

Here, you'll discover recipes that transform the cumbersome duty of daily cooking into a swift, enjoyable process. We'll journey through quick weeknight meals where convenience meets taste without a compromise in nutrition. Think of a savory grilled chicken with a side of aromatic, herb-infused cauliflower rice, or a pan-seared salmon topped with a dollop of dill cream sauce, each dish ready to serve in a matter of minutes.

Expanding beyond the quick fixes, this chapter also explores how you can use your slow cooker to meld flavors slowly, enriching your meals with minimal effort. These recipes ensure that you can enjoy deeply satisfying dinners after a long day's work, ready as soon as you step through the door.

And for times when the calendar marks a special occasion, or when guests are arriving, impressing them won't require culinary feats that keep you tethered to the kitchen all day. You'll learn to craft dishes that are as spectacular to behold as they are delectable to taste—meals that impress without stress.

"Dinner Delights" is designed to make your evenings a little less hectic and a lot more pleasurable. Each recipe is a stepping-stone towards maintaining your low-Carb Composition, high-Protein Composition diet while indulging in the simple pleasure of good food. So, let's turn the page and start creating evenings that are as nourishing as they are delightful.

ZESTY LIME SHRIMP AND AVOCADO SALAD

PREP.TIME: 15 min

COOK.TIME: 0 min

METHOD OF COOK.: No Cooking

SERVES: 4

INGR: 1 lb. shrimp, peeled and deveined

- 2 avocados, diced

- 1 cup cherry tomatoes, halved

- ¼ cup red onion, finely chopped

- 1 jalapeno, seeded and finely chopped

- Juice of 2 limes

- 2 Tbls olive oil

- ¼ cup cilantro, chopped

- Salt and pepper to taste

PROC: Combine shrimp, avocados, cherry tomatoes, red onion, and jalapeno in a large bowl

- In a separate small bowl, whisk together lime juice, olive oil, cilantro, salt, and pepper

- Pour dressing over shrimp mixture and toss gently to combine

TIPS: Serve immediately for best freshness or chill for an hour to enhance flavors

- To increase Protein Composition, add a scoop of cooked quinoa or a handful of chopped walnuts

N.V.: Caloric Content: 290, Fat Composition: 22g, Carb Compositions: 12g, Protein Composition: 17g, Total Sugar: 2g

BEEF AND BROCCOLI STIR-FRY

PREP.TIME: 10 min

COOK.TIME: 10 min

METHOD OF COOK.: Stir-Frying

SERVES: 3

INGR: 1 lb. lean beef strips

- 2 cups broccoli florets

- 1 Tbls coconut oil

- 3 Tbls soy sauce, low sodium

- 1 Tbls sesame oil

- 2 garlic cloves, minced

- 1 Tbls ginger, grated

- 1 tsp erythritol

- Sesame seeds for garnish

PROC: Heat coconut oil in a large skillet over medium-high heat

- Add beef strips and stir-fry until browned and nearly cooked through

- Add broccoli, garlic, and ginger, cooking until vegetables are tender

- Stir in soy sauce, sesame oil, and erythritol and cook for another 2 min.

- Garnish with sesame seeds

TIPS: Serve over a bed of cauliflower rice for a complete meal

- Leftovers make a great lunch option the next day

- Adjust soy sauce quantity for a less salty dish

N.V.: Caloric Content: 325, Fat Composition: 18g, Carb Compositions: 10g, Protein Composition: 30g, Total Sugar: 3g

GARLIC BUTTER SHRIMP WITH ZOODLES

PREP.TIME: 10 mins

COOK.TIME: 15 mins

METHOD OF COOK.: Stovetop

SERVES: 4

INGR: 1 lb. large shrimp, peeled and deveined

- 2 Tbls butter

- 2 cloves garlic, minced

- 1 C. cherry tomatoes, halved

- 3 medium zucchinis, spiralized into noodles

- ¼ tsp red pepper flakes

- Salt and pepper to taste

- Fresh parsley, chopped for garnish

PROC: In a large skillet, melt butter over medium heat and add garlic, cooking until fragrant

- Add shrimp, season with salt, pepper, and red pepper flakes, and cook until shrimp are pink and opaque, about 3-4 minutes per side

- Stir in cherry tomatoes and cook for another 2 minutes

- Add zoodles and toss to coat, cooking just until noodles are slightly tender, about 2 minutes

- Serve immediately, garnished with fresh parsley

TIPS: Add a squeeze of lemon juice for brightness - For added crunch, top with toasted pine nuts

N.V.: Caloric Content: 220, Fat Composition: 12g, Carb Compositions: 5g, Protein Composition: 25g, Total Sugar: 3g

SALMON WITH CREAMY DILL SAUCE

PREP.TIME: 5 min
COOK.TIME: 15 min
METHOD OF COOK.: Baking
SERVES: 4

INGR: 4 salmon fillets, about 6 oz. each

- 1 Tbls olive oil

- Salt and black pepper

- ½ cup Greek yogurt

- 1 Tbls dill, chopped

- 1 tsp lemon zest

- 1 Tbls lemon juice

- 1 garlic clove, minced

PROC: Preheat oven to 400°F (200°C)

- Season salmon with olive oil, salt, and pepper, and place on a lined baking tray

- Bake for 15 min.

- While baking, mix Greek yogurt, dill, lemon zest, lemon juice, and garlic to make the sauce

- Serve salmon with sauce drizzled on top

TIPS: This dish pairs well with a side of steamed asparagus

- For a thinner sauce, add a tablespoon of water or olive oil

N.V.: Caloric Content: 304, Fat Composition: 18g, Carb Compositions: 3g, Protein Composition: 31g, Total Sugar: 2g

CAULIFLOWER STEAK WITH ALMOND PESTO

PREP.TIME: 10 min
COOK.TIME: 20 min
METHOD OF COOK.: Roasting
SERVES: 2

INGR: 1 large cauliflower, sliced into ½-inch thick steaks

- 2 Tbls olive oil

- Salt and pepper to taste

- ½ cup almonds, toasted and crushed

- 1 cup fresh basil leaves

- ¼ cup parmesan cheese, grated

- 2 Tbls olive oil

- 1 garlic clove, minced

PROC: Preheat oven to 425°F (220°C)

- Brush cauliflower steaks with olive oil and season with salt and pepper

- Roast for 20 min.

- For the pesto, blend almonds, basil, parmesan, olive oil, and garlic in a food processor until smooth

- Serve pesto over roasted cauliflower steaks

TIPS: For added Protein Composition, sprinkle roasted chickpeas on top

- Store leftover pesto in the fridge for up to a week

N.V.: Caloric Content: 295, Fat Composition: 25g, Carb Compositions: 10g, Protein Composition: 11g, Total Sugar: 4g

CHICKEN PICCATA WITH CAPERS

PREP.TIME: 15 min

COOK.TIME: 20 min

METHOD OF COOK.: Sautéing

SERVES: 4

INGR: 4 boneless chicken breasts, pounded thin

- 2 Tbls olive oil

- ½ cup chicken broth

- 1 lemon, juiced

- ¼ cup capers

- ¼ cup parsley, chopped

- Salt and pepper to taste

PROC: Heat olive oil in a skillet over medium-high heat

- Season chicken breasts with salt and pepper and sauté until golden and cooked through

- Remove chicken and set aside

- To the same skillet, add chicken broth, lemon juice, and capers, and simmer until the sauce reduces by half

- Return chicken to the skillet and coat with the sauce before serving

TIPS: Garnish with chopped parsley

- Enhance the flavor by adding a splash of white wine to the sauce

N.V.: Caloric Content: 276, Fat Composition: 15g, Carb Compositions: 4g, Protein Composition: 31g, Total Sugar: 1g

PORK CHOPS WITH APPLE CIDER VINEGAR SAUCE

PREP.TIME: 15 min

COOK.TIME: 15 min

METHOD OF COOK.: Grilling

SERVES: 4

INGR: 4 pork chops, bone-in

- 2 Tbls olive oil

- Salt and pepper

- 1 cup apple cider vinegar

- 2 Tbls mustard

- 1 Tbls honey

- 1 apple, sliced

- 1 onion, sliced

PROC: Season pork chops with salt and pepper and brush with olive oil

- Grill over medium heat for 7 min. per side or until fully cooked

- For the sauce, combine apple cider vinegar, mustard, and honey in a pan and simmer until thickened

- Add apple and onion slices until tender

- Serve pork chops with sauce spooned over the top

TIPS: Try serving with a side of roasted brussels sprouts for a complete meal

- The sauce can also be used with chicken or beef

N.V.: Caloric Content: 320, Fat Composition: 18g, Carb Compositions: 15g, Protein Composition: 25g, Total Sugar: 12g

GARLIC PARMESAN CRUSTED CHICKEN

PREP.TIME: 10 mins

COOK.TIME: 20 mins

METHOD OF COOK.: Oven Baking

SERVES: 4

INGR: 4 boneless, skinless chicken breasts

- ½ C. grated Parmesan cheese

- ¼ C. almond flour

- 1 tsp garlic powder

- 1 tsp Italian seasoning

- Salt and pepper to taste

- 2 Tbls olive oil

PROC: Preheat oven to 400°F (200°C)

- In a bowl, combine Parmesan cheese, almond flour, garlic powder, Italian seasoning, salt, and pepper

- Rub chicken breasts with olive oil, then coat them in the Parmesan mixture, pressing gently to adhere

- Place on a baking sheet lined with parchment paper and bake for 20 minutes,

or until chicken is golden and cooked through

- Serve warm

TIPS: For extra flavor, add a sprinkle of fresh parsley on top - Pair with a side of steamed broccoli or cauliflower rice

N.V.: Caloric Content: 280, Fat Composition: 16g, Carb Compositions: 3g, Protein Composition: 32g, Total Sugar: 0g

LEMON GARLIC SHRIMP STIR-FRY

PREP.TIME: 10 mins

COOK.TIME: 15 mins

METHOD OF COOK.: Stovetop

SERVES: 4

INGR: 1 lb. large shrimp, peeled and deveined

- 1 Tbls olive oil

- 1 small zucchini, sliced

- 1 yellow bell pepper, sliced

- 2 cloves garlic, minced

- 1 Tbls lemon juice

- Salt and pepper to taste

- Fresh parsley, chopped for garnish

PROC: Heat olive oil in a large skillet over medium-high heat

- Add garlic and cook until fragrant

- Add shrimp, season with salt and pepper, and cook until pink, about 2-3 minutes per side

- Remove shrimp and set aside

- In the same skillet, add zucchini and bell pepper, cooking until just tender

- Return shrimp to the skillet, add lemon juice, and toss to combine

- Serve immediately with fresh parsley

TIPS: For added zest, garnish with lemon zest - Serve over a bed of spiralized zucchini for a light meal

N.V.: Caloric Content: 220, Fat Composition: 10g, Carb Compositions: 5g, Protein Composition: 25g, Total Sugar: 1g

SPICY TURKEY LETTUCE WRAPS

PREP.TIME: 10 mins

COOK.TIME: 15 mins

METHOD OF COOK.: Stovetop

SERVES: 4

INGR: 1 lb. ground turkey

- 1 Tbls sesame oil

- 1 red bell pepper, diced

- 2 green onions, chopped

- 2 Tbls soy sauce (or tamari for gluten-free)

- 1 tsp chili paste (optional)

- 1 head of romaine lettuce, leaves separated

- Salt and pepper to taste

PROC: In a large skillet, heat sesame oil over medium heat and cook ground turkey until browned

- Add bell pepper, green onions, soy sauce, chili paste, salt, and pepper, stirring well

- Cook for another 5 minutes until peppers are tender

- Spoon mixture into lettuce leaves and serve warm

TIPS: Top with a sprinkle of sesame seeds for extra crunch - Add a dash of lime juice for freshness

N.V.: Caloric Content: 210, Fat Composition: 12g, Carb Compositions: 6g, Protein Composition: 22g, Total Sugar: 2g

BALSAMIC GLAZED BEEF TENDERLOIN

PREP.TIME: 10 mins

COOK.TIME: 20 mins

METHOD OF COOK.: Oven Baking

SERVES: 4

INGR: 1 lb. beef tenderloin

- 2 Tbls balsamic vinegar

- 1 Tbls olive oil

- 1 Tbls fresh rosemary, chopped

- 1 tsp garlic powder

- Salt and pepper to taste

PROC: Preheat oven to 400°F (200°C)

- Rub tenderloin with olive oil, rosemary, garlic powder, salt, and pepper

- Sear in a hot skillet for 2 minutes on each side

- Transfer to a baking dish, brush with balsamic vinegar, and roast for 15-18 minutes for medium-rare

- Rest for 5 minutes before slicing

- Serve with remaining glaze

TIPS: Add a garnish of fresh rosemary for an elegant touch - Serve with a side of roasted Brussels sprouts

N.V.: Caloric Content: 300, Fat Composition: 18g, Carb Compositions: 3g, Protein Composition: 28g, Total Sugar: 1g

LEMON BUTTER SCALLOPS

PREP.TIME: 10 mins

COOK.TIME: 10 mins

METHOD OF COOK.: Stovetop

SERVES: 4

INGR: 1 lb. sea scallops

- 2 Tbls butter

- Zest and juice of 1 lemon

- Salt and pepper to taste

- Fresh parsley, chopped for garnish

PROC: Pat scallops dry and season with salt and pepper

- Heat butter in a large skillet over medium-high heat

- Add scallops and cook 2-3 minutes per side until golden

- Remove scallops, add lemon juice and zest to the pan, stirring to combine with butter

- Pour lemon butter sauce over scallops and garnish with parsley

- Serve immediately

TIPS: Serve with a side of sautéed spinach for color - Use clarified butter for a richer flavor

N.V.: Caloric Content: 240, Fat Composition: 16g, Carb Compositions: 3g, Protein Composition: 20g, Total Sugar: 0g

STUFFED CHICKEN BREAST WITH SPINACH AND FETA

PREP.TIME: 10 mins

COOK.TIME: 20 mins

METHOD OF COOK.: Oven Baking

SERVES: 4

INGR: 4 boneless, skinless chicken breasts

- ½ C. fresh spinach, chopped

- ¼ C. feta cheese, crumbled

- 2 Tbls olive oil

- 1 tsp garlic powder

- Salt and pepper to taste

PROC: Preheat oven to 375°F (190°C)

- Cut a pocket into each chicken breast and stuff with spinach and feta

- Rub the outside with olive oil, garlic powder, salt, and pepper

- Place on a baking sheet and bake for 20 minutes until golden and cooked through

- Serve warm

TIPS: Pair with a side of cauliflower mash for a complete meal - Add a sprinkle of fresh basil for added flavor

N.V.: Caloric Content: 290, Fat Composition: 14g, Carb Compositions: 2g, Protein Composition: 36g, Total Sugar: 0g

HERB-CRUSTED SALMON WITH DIJON SAUCE

PREP.TIME: 10 mins

COOK.TIME: 15 mins

METHOD OF COOK.: Oven Baking

SERVES: 4

INGR: 4 salmon fillets

- 2 Tbls Dijon mustard

- 1 Tbls fresh dill, chopped

- 1 Tbls fresh parsley, chopped

- 1 Tbls olive oil

- Salt and pepper to taste

PROC: Preheat oven to 400°F (200°C)

- Place salmon fillets on a baking sheet, season with salt and pepper

- Spread Dijon mustard over each fillet and sprinkle with dill and parsley

- Drizzle with olive oil and bake for 12-15 minutes until salmon flakes easily

- Serve with Dijon sauce from the pan

TIPS: Serve with roasted asparagus for a balanced dish - Add a sprinkle of lemon zest for brightness

N.V.: Caloric Content: 280, Fat Composition: 18g, Carb Compositions: 1g, Protein Composition: 24g, Total Sugar: 0g

SEARED SCALLOPS WITH CAULIFLOWER PUREE

PREP.TIME: 15 min.

COOK.TIME: 10 min.

METHOD OF COOK.: Pan Searing

SERVES: 4

INGR: 12 large sea scallops, patted dry

- 1 Tbls olive oil

- 2 C. cauliflower florets

- 1 garlic clove, minced

- ½ C. chicken broth

- 2 Tbls unsalted butter

- Salt and pepper to taste

- Fresh parsley, chopped for garnish

PROC: Heat olive oil in a large skillet over medium-high heat

- Add scallops and sear for about 2 min. on each side or until golden brown

- Simultaneously, steam cauliflower until tender

- Blend steamed cauliflower, garlic, chicken broth, and butter until smooth

- Season puree with salt and pepper

- Serve scallops over cauliflower puree

- Garnish with parsley

TIPS: Use a paper towel to ensure scallops are very dry to get a good sear

- Don't overcrowd the pan while searing scallops for even cooking

N.V.: Caloric Content: 200, Fat Composition: 10g, Carb Compositions: 8g, Protein Composition: 20g, Total Sugar: 2g

HERB-CRUSTED RACK OF LAMB

PREP.TIME: 10 mins

COOK.TIME: 20 mins

METHOD OF COOK.: Oven Baking

SERVES: 4

INGR: 1 rack of lamb (about 1.5 lb.), trimmed

- 2 Tbls olive oil

- 2 cloves garlic, minced

- 1 Tbls fresh rosemary, chopped

- 1 Tbls fresh thyme, chopped

- Salt and pepper to taste

PROC: Preheat oven to 400°F (200°C)

- Rub lamb rack with olive oil, then season with garlic, rosemary, thyme, salt, and pepper

- Place lamb on a baking sheet and roast for 20 minutes or until the internal temperature reaches 135°F (57°C) for medium-rare

- Let rest for 5 minutes before slicing

- Serve warm

TIPS: Pair with roasted asparagus for a complete meal - Garnish with a sprinkle of sea salt for enhanced flavor

N.V.: Caloric Content: 320, Fat Composition: 24g, Carb Compositions: 1g, Protein Composition: 25g, Total Sugar: 0g

PROSCIUTTO-WRAPPED COD WITH LEMON CREAM SAUCE

PREP.TIME: 10 mins

COOK.TIME: 15 mins

METHOD OF COOK.: Stovetop

SERVES: 4

INGR: 4 cod fillets (about 4 oz. each)

- 4 slices prosciutto

- 1 Tbls butter

- 1 Tbls olive oil

- 1 Tbls lemon juice

- ¼ C. heavy cream

- Salt and pepper to taste

- Fresh parsley, chopped for garnish

PROC: Wrap each cod fillet with a slice of prosciutto

- In a large skillet, heat butter and olive oil over medium heat

- Add wrapped cod and cook 3-4 minutes per side until prosciutto is crispy and cod is opaque

- Remove cod from the skillet and keep warm

- In the same skillet, add lemon juice and heavy cream, stirring until slightly thickened

- Pour sauce over cod and garnish with parsley

TIPS: Serve with steamed broccoli or a side salad for a balanced dish - For extra lemony flavor, add a bit of zest to the sauce

N.V.: Caloric Content: 280, Fat Composition: 18g, Carb Compositions: 2g, Protein Composition: 24g, Total Sugar: 0g

MEDITERRANEAN SHRIMP SKILLET

PREP.TIME: 10 min.

COOK.TIME: 10 min.

METHOD OF COOK.: Sauteing

SERVES: 4

INGR: 1 lb. large shrimp, peeled and deveined

- 1 Tbls olive oil

- 1 zucchini, sliced

- 1 bell pepper, sliced

- 1/2 C. Kalamata olives, pitted

- 1/4 C. feta cheese, crumbled

- 1 tsp dried oregano

- Salt and pepper to taste

PROC: Heat olive oil in a skillet over medium-high heat

- Add shrimp and vegetables, sauté until shrimp are pink and vegetables are tender

- Season with oregano, salt, and pepper

- Stir in olives and feta cheese just before serving

TIPS: Serve hot with a squeeze of fresh lemon for an added zest

- Can be served over cauliflower rice for a fulfilling low-Carb Composition meal

N.V.: Caloric Content: 215, Fat Composition: 12g, Carb Compositions: 6g, Protein Composition: 23g, Total Sugar: 3g

LEMON GARLIC BUTTER FLANK STEAK

PREP.TIME: 15 min.
COOK.TIME: 10 min.
METHOD OF COOK.: Grilling
SERVES: 4
INGR: 1½ lb. flank steak

- 2 Tbls butter

- 1 lemon, juiced

- 3 garlic cloves, minced

- Salt and pepper to taste

- Fresh parsley, chopped for garnish

PROC: Preheat grill to high heat

- Season steak with salt and pepper

- Grill steak to desired doneness, about 5 min. per side for medium-rare

- Melt butter in a saucepan, add garlic and lemon juice, simmer until fragrant

- Slice steak across the grain, pour lemon garlic butter over it, garnish with parsley

TIPS: Rest steak for 5 min. before slicing to maximize juiciness

- Serve with a low-Carb Composition side like sautéed spinach

N.V.: Caloric Content: 280, Fat Composition: 15g, Carb Compositions: 1g, Protein Composition: 33g, Total Sugar: 0g

SPICY GRILLED TOFU WITH AVOCADO SALSA

PREP.TIME: 15 min.
COOK.TIME: 8 min.
METHOD OF COOK.: Grilling
SERVES: 4
INGR: 1 block firm tofu, pressed and sliced

- 2 Tbls olive oil

- 1 tsp chili powder

- 1 tsp cumin

- 1 avocado, diced

- 1 tomato, diced

- 1 small red onion, finely chopped

- 1 lime, juiced

- Salt and pepper to taste

- Fresh cilantro, chopped for garnish

PROC: Preheat grill to medium-high heat

- Mix olive oil, chili powder, and cumin, brush over tofu slices

- Grill tofu until charred, about 4 min. per side

- Combine avocado, tomato, onion, lime juice, salt, and pepper to make salsa

- Serve grilled tofu topped with avocado salsa and garnished with cilantro

TIPS: Ensure tofu is well-pressed to remove excess water for better texture

- Chili intensity can be adjusted according to taste preferences

- A perfect dish for vegans seeking high-Protein Composition meals

N.V.: Caloric Content: 220, Fat Composition: 15g, Carb Compositions: 9g, Protein Composition: 12g, Total Sugar: 2g

8. LOW-CARB COMPOSITION DESSERTS

Indulging in a sweet treat while maintaining a low-Carb Composition, high-Protein Composition diet often feels like a culinary paradox. However, I've crafted this chapter to dismantle the belief that desserts need to be off-limits when you're committed to a healthier lifestyle. This serendipitous journey into low-Carb Composition desserts will not only satisfy your sweet tooth but also align with your dietary goals, ensuring you can enjoy the sweeter side of life without compromise.

Many fear that transitioning to a low-Carb Composition lifestyle means saying a permanent goodbye to desserts. Let me assure you, it's quite the contrary. With the right ingredients and a bit of creativity, you can recreate those beloved flavors in forms that are both nourishing and indulgent. Whether it's the rich, silky texture of a chocolate mousse or the crisp, satisfying crunch of a homemade cookie, this chapter provides recipes that you can savor without guilt.

Imagine savoring a slice of creamy cheesecake that aligns perfectly with your dietary needs. Or picture enjoying a scoop of frosty, homemade ice cream that doesn't send your Carb Composition count soaring. These aren't just daydreams; they are real, attainable dessert options fashioned for your low-Carb Composition regimen. Each recipe in this segment is designed to embrace the natural sweetness of its ingredients, reducing the need for added Total Sugars and maximizing the nutritional impact.

The brilliance of these desserts lies not only in their flavors but in their simplicity. Time, as we know, is a precious commodity. Therefore, I have ensured that these dessert recipes are as straightforward as they are swift, allowing you to whip up impressive treats for yourself and your loved ones without laboring for hours in the kitchen.

By the end of this chapter, the world of low-Carb Composition desserts will open up to you as a delightful new aspect of your culinary repertoire, proving once and for all that healthy eating does not need to be restrictive or mundane. Indulgence, satisfaction, and health coexist beautifully in each recipe, promising delights that will not only bewitch your palate but also bolster your wellness journey.

COCONUT FLOUR SHORTBREAD COOKIES

PREP.TIME: 15 min
COOK.TIME: 12 min
METHOD OF COOK.: Baking
SERVES: 16
INGR: 2 C. almond flour

- ½ C. coconut flour

- ⅓ C. erythritol

- ½ C. unsalted butter, softened

- 1 tsp vanilla extract

- 1 large egg

PROC: Preheat oven to 350°F (175°C)

- In a mixing bowl, combine almond flour, coconut flour, and erythritol

- Add softened butter, vanilla extract, and egg and mix until a dough forms

- Roll dough into 1-inch balls and flatten to form cookies on a parchment-lined baking sheet

- Bake until edges are golden brown

TIPS: Chill dough for 30 minutes before baking for easier handling

- Use cookie stamps to imprint designs before baking

N.V.: Caloric Content: 130, Fat Composition: 11g, Carb Compositions: 4g, Protein Composition: 3g, Total Sugar: 1g

LEMON POPPY SEED PROTEIN COMPOSITION CAKES

PREP.TIME: 10 min
COOK.TIME: 18 min
METHOD OF COOK.: Baking
SERVES: 12
INGR: 1 C. almond flour

- 2 Tbls coconut flour

- ¼ C. vanilla whey Protein Composition powder

- ½ tsp baking powder

- 3 Tbls poppy seeds

- 2 large eggs

- ¼ C. Greek yogurt

- ¼ C. erythritol

- Zest and juice of 1 lemon

- ¼ C. unsweetened almond milk

PROC: Preheat oven to 375°F (190°C)

- Mix almond flour, coconut flour, Protein Composition powder, baking powder, and poppy seeds in a bowl

- In another bowl, whisk eggs, Greek yogurt, erythritol, lemon zest, lemon juice, and almond milk

- Combine wet and dry ingredients gently

- Spoon into lined muffin tins and bake until a toothpick comes out clean

TIPS: Add extra lemon zest on top before baking for a zesty finish

- Store in an airtight container to maintain freshness

N.V.: Caloric Content: 145, Fat Composition: 9g, Carb Compositions: 8g, Protein Composition: 7g, Total Sugar: 2g

ALMOND JOY COOKIES

PREP.TIME: 20 min
COOK.TIME: 15 min
METHOD OF COOK.: Baking
SERVES: 24
INGR: 1½ C. almond flour

- 1 tsp baking powder

- ½ tsp salt

- ⅓ C. coconut oil, melted

- ½ C. erythritol

- 1 large egg

- 1 tsp almond extract

- ½ C. unsweetened shredded coconut

- ¼ C. Total Sugar-free dark chocolate chips

- ¼ C. chopped almonds

PROC: Preheat oven to 350°F (175°C)

- Whisk together almond flour, baking powder, and salt in a large bowl

- In a separate bowl, mix melted coconut oil, erythritol, egg, and almond extract until smooth

- Stir wet ingredients into dry ingredients

- Fold in coconut, chocolate chips, and almonds

- Drop tablespoons of dough onto a baking sheet and bake until golden

TIPS: Press additional chocolate chips and almond pieces on top before baking for aesthetic appeal

- Keep cookies refrigerated to enhance flavor and texture

N.V.: Caloric Content: 135, Fat Composition: 11g, Carb Compositions: 5g, Protein Composition: 4g, Total Sugar: 1g

SPICED CHAI PROTEIN COMPOSITION COOKIES

PREP.TIME: 18 min

COOK.TIME: 12 min

METHOD OF COOK.: Baking

SERVES: 15

INGR: 1 C. almond flour

- ¼ C. pea Protein Composition powder

- 1 tsp ground cinnamon

- ½ tsp ground cardamom

- ¼ tsp ground nutmeg

- ¼ tsp ground ginger

- Pinch of black pepper

- ⅓ C. butter, softened

- ¼ C. erythritol

- 1 large egg

- 1 tsp vanilla extract

PROC: Preheat oven to 350°F (175°C)

- Combine almond flour, Protein Composition powder, spices, and pepper in a bowl

- In another bowl, cream together butter and erythritol until fluffy

- Beat in egg and vanilla

- Gradually mix dry ingredients into wet until a dough forms

- Shape into cookies and place on a baking sheet

- Bake until edges are slightly browned

TIPS: Roll dough balls in a mixture of cinnamon and erythritol before baking for added spice

- Allow cookies to cool on the baking sheet for 5 minutes before transferring to a wire rack

N.V.: Caloric Content: 125, Fat Composition: 9g, Carb Compositions: 4g, Protein Composition: 5g, Total Sugar: 1g

CHOCOLATE WALNUT ESPRESSO COOKIES

PREP.TIME: 15 min

COOK.TIME: 12 min

METHOD OF COOK.: Baking

SERVES: 20

INGR: 1 C. walnuts, finely ground

- ½ C. almond flour

- ⅓ C. cocoa powder

- 1 tsp espresso powder

- ½ tsp baking soda

- ⅓ C. coconut oil, melted

- ½ C. erythritol

- 1 egg

- 1 tsp vanilla extract

PROC: Preheat oven to 350°F (175°C)

- Mix ground walnuts, almond flour, cocoa powder, espresso powder, and baking soda in a bowl

- In another bowl, whisk together melted coconut oil, erythritol, egg, and vanilla extract

- Combine wet and dry ingredients and stir until a cohesive dough forms

- Place teaspoonfuls on a cookie sheet and flatten slightly

- Bake until set

TIPS: Add a pinch of sea salt to the dough for a flavor contrast

- These cookies are best enjoyed with a cup of strong coffee

N.V.: Caloric Content: 110, Fat Composition: 9g, Carb Compositions: 4g, Protein Composition: 3g, Total Sugar: 1g

PUMPKIN SPICE PROTEIN COMPOSITION COOKIES

PREP.TIME: 20 min

COOK.TIME: 15 min

METHOD OF COOK.: Baking

SERVES: 18

INGR: 1 C. almond flour

- ¼ C. vanilla Protein Composition powder

- 1 tsp pumpkin pie spice

- ½ tsp baking powder

- ¼ C. canned pumpkin puree

- ¼ C. butter, softened

- ⅓ C. erythritol

- 1 Tbls flaxseed meal (mixed with 3 Tbls water and set aside for 5 minutes to thicken)

PROC: Preheat oven to 375°F (190°C)

- Mix almond flour, Protein Composition powder, pumpkin pie spice, and baking powder in a bowl

- In another bowl, cream butter and erythritol

- Gradually add pumpkin puree and flaxseed mixture to butter mix

- Combine wet and dry ingredients

- Drop spoonfuls on a baking sheet, flatten slightly

- Bake until edges are lightly browned

TIPS: Sprinkle some raw pumpkin seeds on top before baking for extra crunch

- Store in an airtight container to keep cookies moist

N.V.: Caloric Content: 140, Fat Composition: 10g, Carb Compositions: 6g, Protein Composition: 5g, Total Sugar: 1g

SNICKERDOODLE PROTEIN COMPOSITION COOKIES

PREP.TIME: 15 min

COOK.TIME: 10 min

METHOD OF COOK.: Baking

SERVES: 24

INGR: 1 C. almond flour

- ⅓ C. vanilla whey Protein Composition powder

- ½ tsp cream of tartar

- ¼ tsp baking soda

- ¼ tsp salt

- ½ C. butter, softened

- ⅓ C. erythritol

- 1 large egg

- 1 tsp vanilla extract

- 2 Tbls granulated erythritol

- 1 tsp cinnamon for rolling

PROC: Preheat oven to 350°F (175°C)

- Mix almond flour, Protein Composition powder, cream of tartar, baking soda, and salt in a bowl

- In another bowl, cream butter and erythritol

- Beat in egg and vanilla extract

- Gradually mix dry ingredients into wet until a dough forms

- Combine granulated erythritol and cinnamon in a small bowl

- Form dough into balls, roll in cinnamon mixture, and place on baking sheet

- Flatten slightly and bake until edges are set

TIPS: Try dipping half of each cookie in melted Total Sugar-free chocolate after they cool for a decadent touch

- Handle dough with cool hands to prevent sticking

N.V.: Caloric Content: 130, Fat Composition: 10g, Carb Compositions: 3g, Protein Composition: 5g, Total Sugar: 1g

VANILLA MASCARPONE MOUSSE

PREP.TIME: 15 min

COOK.TIME: 0 min

METHOD OF COOK.: No Cooking

SERVES: 4

INGR: 8 oz. mascarpone cheese

- 1 C. heavy cream

- 1 tsp vanilla extract

- 1/4 C. erythritol

- 2 Tbls unsweetened gelatin powder, dissolved in 1/4 C. boiling water

PROC: Combine mascarpone, heavy cream, vanilla, and erythritol in a bowl and beat until smooth

- Add dissolved gelatin to the mixture and beat until light and fluffy

- Spoon into serving dishes and refrigerate until set

TIPS: Serve with a sprinkle of cinnamon or nutmeg for added flavor

- Top with a few fresh berries for a burst of color and taste

N.V.: Caloric Content: 310, Fat Composition: 30g, Carb Compositions: 4g, Protein Composition: 5g, Total Sugar: 2g

CHOCOLATE AVOCADO SILK PIE

PREP.TIME: 20 min

COOK.TIME: 0 min

METHOD OF COOK.: No Cooking

SERVES: 8

INGR: 2 ripe avocados, peeled and pitted

- 1/2 C. cocoa powder

- 1/3 C. coconut oil, melted

- 1/2 C. erythritol

- 1 tsp vanilla extract

- 1 prepared almond flour pie crust

PROC: Blend avocados, cocoa powder, coconut oil, erythritol, and vanilla in a food processor until smooth

- Pour mixture into pie crust and smooth the top

- Chill in the refrigerator for at least 2 hrs

TIPS: Decorate with unsweetened whipped cream and chocolate shavings before serving

- Keep pie chilled until ready to serve for best texture

N.V.: Caloric Content: 275, Fat Composition: 25g, Carb Compositions: 12g, Protein Composition: 4g, Total Sugar: 1g

LEMON RICOTTA PARFAIT

PREP.TIME: 10 min

COOK.TIME: 0 min

METHOD OF COOK.: No Cooking

SERVES: 4

INGR: 1 C. ricotta cheese

- 1/2 C. Greek yogurt, full-Fat Composition

- Zest of 1 lemon

- 2 Tbls lemon juice

- 1/4 C. erythritol

- 1/4 tsp vanilla extract

- Almond flakes, toasted for garnish

PROC: Mix ricotta, Greek yogurt, lemon zest, lemon juice, erythritol, and vanilla extract until well combined

- Layer the mixture with toasted almond flakes in glasses

- Chill before serving

TIPS: Garnish with fresh mint for a refreshing touch

- Use a ribbon of lemon peel as decoration for an elegant presentation

N.V.: Caloric Content: 200, Fat Composition: 15g, Carb Compositions: 8g, Protein Composition: 9g, Total Sugar: 3g

STRAWBERRY COCONUT CREAM POTS

PREP.TIME: 10 min

COOK.TIME: 0 min

METHOD OF COOK.: No Cooking

SERVES: 6

INGR: 2 C. strawberries, chopped

- 1 C. coconut cream

- 1/4 C. erythritol

- 1 tsp vanilla extract

- Fresh strawberries for topping

PROC: Combine chopped strawberries, coconut cream, erythritol, and vanilla extract in a blender and blend until smooth

- Pour into small serving bowls or glasses

- Top with fresh strawberries and chill until serving

TIPS: Opt for organic strawberries for more natural sweetness

- Chill thoroughly to allow flavors to meld beautifully

N.V.: Caloric Content: 180, Fat Composition: 14g, Carb Compositions: 10g, Protein Composition: 2g, Total Sugar: 5g

PEANUT BUTTER MOUSSE

PREP.TIME: 15 min

COOK.TIME: 0 min

METHOD OF COOK.: No Cooking

SERVES: 4

INGR: 1/2 C. natural peanut butter

- 1 C. whipped cream

- 1/4 C. erythritol

- Dark chocolate shavings for garnish

PROC: Whip the cream with erythritol until stiff peaks form

- Gently fold in the peanut butter until well combined

- Spoon into serving dishes and garnish with chocolate shavings

- Chill before serving

TIPS: Select a peanut butter with no added Total Sugar for a healthier option

- Serve with a sprinkle of sea salt on top to enhance flavors

N.V.: Caloric Content: 295, Fat Composition: 25g, Carb Compositions: 8g, Protein Composition: 7g, Total Sugar: 3g

PUMPKIN CHEESECAKE FLUFF

PREP.TIME: 10 min
COOK.TIME: 0 min
METHOD OF COOK.: No Cooking
SERVES: 6
INGR: 15 oz. canned pumpkin puree

- 8 oz. cream cheese, softened

- 1/2 C. heavy cream

- 1/4 C. erythritol

- 1 tsp pumpkin pie spice

- 1/2 tsp vanilla extract

PROC: Whip cream cheese until smooth

- Add pumpkin puree, erythritol, pumpkin pie spice, and vanilla extract and beat until well combined

- In a separate bowl, whip heavy cream and then fold into the pumpkin mixture

- Chill before serving in individual cups

TIPS: Sprinkle with a little extra pumpkin pie spice before serving for a festive touch

- Can be made a day ahead to enhance the flavors

N.V.: Caloric Content: 210, Fat Composition: 18g, Carb Compositions: 9g, Protein Composition: 4g, Total Sugar: 4g

VANILLA BEAN PANNA COTTA

PREP.TIME: 10 mins
COOK.TIME: 0 mins
METHOD OF COOK.: Refrigeration
SERVES: 4

INGR: 1 C. heavy cream

- 1 C. unsweetened almond milk

- 1 Tbls powdered gelatin

- 1 vanilla bean, split and seeds scraped

- 2 Tbls erythritol or monk fruit sweetener

PROC: In a small saucepan, heat the heavy cream, almond milk, vanilla bean seeds, and pod over medium heat until warm (do not boil)

- Remove from heat and whisk in the gelatin and sweetener until dissolved

- Pour mixture into individual ramekins, cover, and refrigerate for at least 4 hours or until set

- Serve chilled

TIPS: Top with a few fresh berries for color

- For extra vanilla flavor, add a few drops of vanilla extract

N.V.: Caloric Content: 180, Fat Composition: 16g, Carb Compositions: 3g, Protein Composition: 5g, Total Sugar: 0g

LEMON COCONUT FREEZE

PREP.TIME: 15 min
COOK.TIME: 0 min
METHOD OF COOK.: No Cooking
SERVES: 8
INGR: 2 C. coconut cream

- zest of 1 lemon

- juice of 1 lemon

- ¼ C. erythritol

- ½ tsp vanilla extract

- pinch of salt

PROC: Combine coconut cream, lemon zest, lemon juice, erythritol, vanilla extract, and salt in a bowl and whisk until smooth

- Pour mixture into an ice cream maker and churn according to the manufacturer's instructions

- Transfer to a freezer-safe container and freeze until firm

TIPS: Use organic lemons for the best flavor

- Serve with fresh mint for an extra zesty kick

N.V.: Caloric Content: 230, Fat Composition: 22g, Carb Compositions: 6g, Protein Composition: 2g, Total Sugar: 1g

RASPBERRY PROTEIN COMPOSITION SORBET

PREP.TIME: 10 min

COOK.TIME: 0 min

METHOD OF COOK.: No Cooking

SERVES: 6

INGR: 2 C. frozen raspberries

- 1 scoop vanilla Protein Composition powder

- ¼ C. almond milk

- 1 Tbls chia seeds

- Erythritol to taste

PROC: Blend frozen raspberries, vanilla Protein Composition powder, almond milk, chia seeds, and erythritol in a high-speed blender until smooth

- Taste and adjust sweetness if necessary

- Serve immediately or freeze for 30 min for a firmer texture

TIPS: Add a splash of lime juice to enhance raspberry flavor

- If too thick, adjust by adding a little more almond milk

N.V.: Caloric Content: 100, Fat Composition: 2g, Carb Compositions: 12g, Protein Composition: 7g, Total Sugar: 3g

CHOCOLATE AVOCADO GELATO

PREP.TIME: 20 min

COOK.TIME: 0 min

METHOD OF COOK.: No Cooking

SERVES: 4

INGR: 1 ripe avocado

- 1/4 C. unsweetened cocoa powder

- 1/2 C. coconut milk

- 1/3 C. erythritol

- 1 tsp almond extract

- pinch of salt

PROC: Blend avocado, cocoa powder, coconut milk, erythritol, almond extract, and salt in a blender until completely smooth

- Pour into a freezer-safe bowl and freeze, stirring every 30 min, until desired consistency is reached

TIPS: Serve with crushed nuts for added texture

- Use ripe avocados for better texture and natural sweetness

N.V.: Caloric Content: 170, Fat Composition: 15g, Carb Compositions: 13g, Protein Composition: 2g, Total Sugar: 1g

MINT MATCHA FROZEN YOGURT

PREP.TIME: 15 min

COOK.TIME: 0 min

METHOD OF COOK.: No Cooking

SERVES: 5

INGR: 2 C. Greek yogurt, strained

- 1 Tbls matcha powder

- 1/4 C. erythritol

- 1 tsp mint extract

- 1/4 C. crushed dark chocolate, Total Sugar-free

PROC: Whisk together Greek yogurt, matcha powder, erythritol, and mint extract until well combined

- Fold in crushed dark chocolate

- Pour the mixture into an ice cream maker and churn according to manufacturer's instructions

TIPS: Opt for full-Fat Composition Greek yogurt for creamier texture

- Garnish with mint leaves for visual appeal and freshness

N.V.: Caloric Content: 140, Fat Composition: 4g, Carb Compositions: 10g, Protein Composition: 19g, Total Sugar: 4g

BLUEBERRY ALMOND ICE DELIGHT

PREP.TIME: 18 min

COOK.TIME: 0 min

METHOD OF COOK.: No Cooking

SERVES: 6

INGR: 1 C. frozen blueberries

- 1/2 C. Greek yogurt

- 1/4 C. sliced almonds, toasted

- 1/4 C. coconut cream

- 1 Tbls erythritol

- 1/2 tsp vanilla extract

PROC: Blend frozen blueberries, Greek yogurt, coconut cream, erythritol, and vanilla extract until smooth

- Stir in toasted sliced almonds

- Freeze in an airtight container for at least 2 hr before serving

TIPS: Choose wild blueberries for more intense flavor

- Toast almonds to enhance their nutty flavor

N.V.: Caloric Content: 120, Fat Composition: 8g, Carb Compositions: 9g, Protein Composition: 4g, Total Sugar: 5g

CINNAMON PECAN CRUNCH FREEZE

PREP.TIME: 10 min

COOK.TIME: 0 min

METHOD OF COOK.: No Cooking

SERVES: 8

INGR: 2 C. heavy cream

- 1/2 C. chopped pecans, toasted

- 2 Tbls ground cinnamon

- 1/3 C. erythritol

- 1 tsp vanilla extract

PROC: Mix heavy cream, erythritol, cinnamon, and vanilla in a bowl until well blended

- Fold in toasted pecans

- Pour into a loaf pan and freeze until solid, stirring occasionally

TIPS: Sprinkle extra cinnamon on top before serving for a stronger flavor

- Serve with a dollop of coconut cream for extra richness

N.V.: Caloric Content: 300, Fat Composition: 30g, Carb Compositions: 5g, Protein Composition: 2g, Total Sugar: 1g

9. CREATIVE SMOOTHIES AND DRINKS

Welcome to a vibrant chapter where your blender becomes your best friend in your culinary adventure toward health and vitality. Picture this: It's early morning, the house is quiet, and you're about to whip up something magical that's both nourishing and delightfully delicious.

Here, we step into the world of creative smoothies and drinks—an essential component of our low Carb Composition, high Protein Composition journey. These concoctions are not just beverages; they are power-packed meals! Whether you're dashing out the door with a portable breakfast smoothie or winding down with a refreshing, Protein Composition-infused drink, each sip is designed to support your health goals while pleasing your palate.

Smoothies and specially crafted drinks are formidable allies in our quest to manage weight and improve overall health. They serve as a perfect vehicle for integrating a variety of nutrients in one go. Consider how a carefully composed smoothie can deliver a rich blend of Protein Composition, healthy Fat Compositions, and fiber—all while keeping the Carb Compositions in check. The versatility doesn't end there; with the right ingredients, a smoothie can double as a meal replacement or a rejuvenating post-workout refreshment.

I understand your daily hustles and the desire to enjoy life without compromising on health or flavor. Hence, this chapter is crafted to arm you with recipes that are as quick to prepare as they are beneficial and enjoyable. Imagine tossing some spinach, a scoop of Protein Composition powder, a hint of avocado, and a splash of almond milk into your blender. In less than five minutes, you have a creamy, satisfying drink that keeps you energized and aligned with your dietary goals.

As we delve into these recipes, remember each ingredient is chosen to not only impart great taste but also to contribute beneficially to your body. Beyond mere sustenance, these drinks are designed to invigorate and inspire a lifestyle change—one delicious sip at a time. So, let's raise our glasses to smart, healthful living that delights as much as it nourishes!

BERRY-WHEY POWER SMOOTHIE

PREP. TIME: 5 min.

COOK. TIME: 0 min.

METHOD OF COOK.: Blending

SERVES: 2

INGR: 1 C. frozen mixed berries

- 1 scoop vanilla whey Protein Composition powder

- 1 C. unsweetened almond milk

- 1 Tbls flaxseeds

- 1 Tbls chia seeds

- ½ small avocado

- Stevia to taste

PROC: Combine all ingredients in blender and blitz until smoothly mixed

- Pour into glasses and serve immediately

TIPS: Add ice for a chilled version

- Blend on high for a smoother texture

N.V.: Caloric Content: 290, Fat Composition: 15g, Carb Compositions: 12g, Protein Composition: 25g, Total Sugar: 4g

GREEN MUSCLE MACHINE

PREP. TIME: 7 min.

COOK. TIME: 0 min.

METHOD OF COOK.: Blending

SERVES: 1

INGR: 1 C. fresh spinach

- 1 scoop plant-based Protein Composition powder, unflavored

- ½ C. cucumber, chopped

- ¼ C. coconut water

- 1 Tbls almond butter

- 1 tsp spirulina powder

- Ice cubes

- Erythritol to taste

PROC: Blend spinach, cucumber, and coconut water until smooth

- Add Protein Composition powder, almond butter, spirulina, and ice, blend until creamy

TIPS: Use frozen spinach for extra coldness

- Sprinkle with hemp seeds for added texture and Protein Composition

N.V.: Caloric Content: 255, Fat Composition: 14g, Carb Compositions: 10g, Protein Composition: 21g, Total Sugar: 2g

KETO AVOCADO-TOFU SMOOTHIE

PREP. TIME: 6 min.

COOK. TIME: 0 min.

METHOD OF COOK.: Blending

SERVES: 1

INGR: ½ medium avocado

- 100g silken tofu

- 1 C. unsweetened cashew milk

- 1 tsp lemon juice

- 1 Tbls MCT oil

- Erythritol to taste

PROC: Place all ingredients into a blender and mix until ultra-smooth

- Serve chilled, garnished with a slice of lemon

TIPS: Opt for organic tofu to ensure non-GMO ingredients

- Add a pinch of pink Himalayan salt to enhance flavors

N.V.: Caloric Content: 400, Fat Composition: 32g, Carb Compositions: 8g, Protein Composition: 18g, Total Sugar: 1g

SUNRISE PROTEIN COMPOSITION BURST

PREP.TIME: 5 min.

COOK.TIME: 0 min.

METHOD OF COOK.: Blending

SERVES: 2

INGR: 1 C. frozen strawberries

- 1 scoop Protein Composition powder, strawberry flavor

- 1 C. Greek yogurt, full-Fat Composition

- ½ C. unsweetened almond milk

- 1 tsp vanilla extract

- Stevia to taste

PROC: Blend all ingredients until smooth and well combined

- Pour into glasses and enjoy immediately

TIPS: Add a splash of flaxseed oil for Omega-3s

- Top with a few whole berries for a delightful presentation

N.V.: Caloric Content: 280, Fat Composition: 9g, Carb Compositions: 15g, Protein Composition: 35g, Total Sugar: 8g

CHOCO-PEANUT BUTTER BLISS

PREP.TIME: 8 min.

COOK.TIME: 0 min.

METHOD OF COOK.: Blending

SERVES: 1

INGR: 1 C. unsweetened almond milk

- 1 Tbls unsweetened cocoa powder

- 1 scoop chocolate Protein Composition powder

- 2 Tbls peanut butter, no added Total Sugar

- 1 Tbls hemp seeds

- Ice cubes

- Stevia to taste

PROC: Blend all ingredients until the texture is silky smooth

- Garnish with a sprinkle of cocoa powder and enjoy

TIPS: Substitute peanut butter with almond butter for a different taste profile

- Serve immediately for best taste and consistency

N.V.: Caloric Content: 340, Fat Composition: 22g, Carb Compositions: 12g, Protein Composition: 28g, Total Sugar: 2g

TROPICAL TURMERIC TONIC

PREP.TIME: 6 min.

COOK.TIME: 0 min.

METHOD OF COOK.: Blending

SERVES: 1

INGR: 1 C. coconut water

- ½ C. frozen mango chunks

- 1 scoop vanilla Protein Composition powder

- 1 Tbls flaxseed oil

- 1 tsp turmeric powder

- 1 tsp lime juice

- Ice cubes

- Stevia to taste

PROC: Blend all ingredients until the mixture is bright and frothy

- Serve in a chilled glass with a slice of lime

TIPS: Add a pinch of black pepper to boost turmeric absorption

- Garnish with mint for a fresh pop of flavor

N.V.: Caloric Content: 260, Fat Composition: 14g, Carb Compositions: 15g, Protein Composition: 20g, Total Sugar: 10g

VANILLA CHAI INFUSION

PREP.TIME: 4 min.

COOK.TIME: 0 min.

METHOD OF COOK.: Blending

SERVES: 2

INGR: 1 C. brewed chai tea, cooled

- 1 scoop vanilla Protein Composition powder

- ½ C. heavy cream

- 1 Tbls almond oil

- ¼ tsp ground cinnamon

- Ice cubes

- Erythritol to taste

PROC: Place all ingredients in blender and pulse until creamy

- Pour into serving glasses and sprinkle with a dash of cinnamon

TIPS: Opt for full-Fat Composition heavy cream to enhance creaminess

- Serve with a cinnamon stick for aromatic appeal

N.V.: Caloric Content: 310, Fat Composition: 26g, Carb Compositions: 5g, Protein Composition: 16g, Total Sugar: 2g

CUCUMBER MINT REFRESHER

PREP.TIME: 5 min

COOK.TIME: 0 min

METHOD OF COOK.: No Cooking

SERVES: 2

INGR: 1 large cucumber, peeled and chopped

- 10 mint leaves

- 1 Tbls fresh lime juice

- 1/2 tsp stevia

- 2 C. cold water

- Ice cubes

PROC: Combine cucumber, mint leaves, lime juice, and stevia in a blender

- Blend until smooth

- Strain the mixture using a fine mesh sieve into a pitcher

- Add cold water and stir well

- Serve over ice

TIPS: Enjoy immediately for the best flavor

- For an extra chill, refrigerate the juice for 1 hr before serving

- Add a splash of sparkling water for a fizzy twist

N.V.: Caloric Content: 8, Fat Composition: 0.1g, Carb Compositions: 2g, Protein Composition: 0.4g, Total Sugar: 1g

SPICY TOMATO TANGO

PREP.TIME: 10 min

COOK.TIME: 0 min

METHOD OF COOK.: No Cooking

SERVES: 2

INGR: 2 large tomatoes, quartered

- 1 small jalapeño, seeds removed

- 1/2 red bell pepper, chopped

- 1 Tbls apple cider vinegar

- 1/2 tsp salt

- 1/2 tsp black pepper

- 1 C. cold water

- Ice cubes

PROC: Place tomatoes, jalapeño, bell pepper, apple cider vinegar, salt, and black pepper in a blender

- Pulse until well combined

- Pour through a fine mesh sieve into a large bowl

- Press solids to extract as much juice as possible

- Mix the strained juice with cold water

- Serve over ice

TIPS: Discard the solids after straining for a clearer juice

- Add a stalk of celery when blending for extra nutrients and flavor

- Adjust the amount of jalapeño for desired spice level

N.V.: Caloric Content: 18, Fat Composition: 0.2g, Carb Compositions: 4g, Protein Composition: 1g, Total Sugar: 3g

GOLDEN GINGER ZINGER

PREP.TIME: 8 min

COOK.TIME: 0 min

METHOD OF COOK.: No Cooking

SERVES: 1

INGR: 1 inch piece of ginger, peeled and sliced

- 1/2 tsp turmeric powder

- Juice of 1 lemon

- 1 Tbls chia seeds

- 1 tsp stevia

- 1 1/2 C. cold water

- Ice cubes

PROC: Combine ginger, turmeric, lemon juice, chia seeds, and stevia in a blender

- Blend until smooth

- Strain through a cheesecloth or fine mesh sieve into a glass

- Add cold water and stir well

- Serve over ice

TIPS: To enhance absorption of turmeric, add a pinch of black pepper to the blend

- Let the mixture sit for 5 min after blending to allow the chia seeds to swell

- A slice of cucumber adds a refreshing twist

N.V.: Caloric Content: 35, Fat Composition: 1.5g, Carb Compositions: 6g, Protein Composition: 2g, Total Sugar: 0g

BERRY BASIL BLAST

PREP.TIME: 7 min

COOK.TIME: 0 min

METHOD OF COOK.: No Cooking

SERVES: 2

INGR: 1 C. mixed fresh berries (blueberries, raspberries, strawberries)

- 5 basil leaves

- 1 Tbls lemon juice

- 1 tsp erythritol

- 2 C. cold water

- Ice cubes

PROC: Combine berries, basil leaves, lemon juice, and erythritol in a blender

- Blend until smooth

- Strain the mixture using a fine mesh sieve into a pitcher

- Add cold water and mix well

- Serve chilled over ice

TIPS: Press basil leaves before adding to release more flavor

- Can add mint for a more complex flavor profile

- Freeze extra berries to use directly in the juice for added chill and flavor

N.V.: Caloric Content: 32, Fat Composition: 0.3g, Carb Compositions: 8g, Protein Composition: 1g, Total Sugar: 5g

AVOCADO LIME COOLER

PREP.TIME: 6 min

COOK.TIME: 0 min

METHOD OF COOK.: No Cooking

SERVES: 1

INGR: 1 ripe avocado, pitted and scooped

- Juice of 1 lime

- 1 Tbls chopped cilantro

- 1/2 tsp stevia

- 1 1/2 C. cold water

- Ice cubes

PROC: Blend avocado, lime juice, cilantro, and stevia in a blender until smooth

- Add cold water and blend again until well mixed

- Serve over ice

TIPS: For a creamier texture, blend longer

- Adding a pinch of salt can enhance the flavors

- Pair with a spicy meal to soothe the palate

N.V.: Caloric Content: 160, Fat Composition: 15g, Carb Compositions: 9g, Protein Composition: 2g, Total Sugar: 0.7g

PINEAPPLE COCONUT HYDRATOR

PREP.TIME: 7 min

COOK.TIME: 0 min

METHOD OF COOK.: No Cooking

SERVES: 2

INGR: 1/2 C. fresh pineapple chunks

- 1/2 C. coconut water

- 1 tsp lime juice

- 1/2 tsp erythritol

- Ice cubes

PROC: Place pineapple, coconut water, lime juice, and erythritol in a blender

- Blend until smooth

- Serve chilled over ice

TIPS: Use fresh pineapple for a sweeter flavor

- For added hydration, replace half of the coconut water with electrolyte-rich water

- To increase Protein Composition, add a scoop of unflavored Protein Composition powder

N.V.: Caloric Content: 46, Fat Composition: 0.3g, Carb Compositions: 11g, Protein Composition: 0.5g, Total Sugar: 8g

KALE LEMONADE DETOX

PREP.TIME: 10 min

COOK.TIME: 0 min

METHOD OF COOK.: No Cooking

SERVES: 1

INGR: 6 large kale leaves, stems removed

- Juice of 2 lemons

- 1 Tbls flaxseed oil

- 1 tsp stevia

- 2 C. cold water

- Ice cubes

PROC: Add kale leaves, lemon juice, flaxseed oil, and stevia to a high-speed blender

- Blend until smooth and frothy

- Mix with cold water

- Serve over ice

TIPS: Remove kale stems for a less bitter taste

- Adding a slice of ginger can provide a warming effect and boost digestion

- Strain through a fine mesh for smoother texture

N.V.: Caloric Content: 130, Fat Composition: 9g, Carb Compositions: 12g, Protein Composition: 3g, Total Sugar: 1g

CINNAMON VANILLA BULLETPROOF COFFEE

PREP.TIME: 5 min

COOK.TIME: 0 min

METHOD OF COOK.: No Cooking

SERVES: 1

INGR: 1 C. brewed coffee

- 1 Tbls unsalted butter

- 2 Tbls coconut oil

- ¼ tsp vanilla extract

- ½ tsp ground cinnamon

- 1 tsp erythritol

PROC: Brew coffee to your liking

- Blend hot coffee, butter, coconut oil, vanilla extract, cinnamon, and erythritol until frothy

TIPS: Try adding a dash of nutmeg for a spicy twist

- This drink is best enjoyed hot

N.V.: Caloric Content: 220, Fat Composition: 24g, Carb Compositions: 1g, Protein Composition: 1g, Total Sugar: 0g

SPICY MOCHA LATTE

PREP.TIME: 10 min

COOK.TIME: 0 min

METHOD OF COOK.: No Cooking

SERVES: 1

INGR: 1 C. brewed coffee

- 1 Tbls cocoa powder

- ¼ tsp cayenne pepper

- 1 Tbls heavy cream

- 1 tsp erythritol

PROC: Blend brewed coffee, cocoa powder, cayenne pepper, heavy cream, and erythritol until smooth and well combined

TIPS: Serve over ice for a refreshing twist

- Adjust cayenne pepper according to your spice preference

N.V.: Caloric Content: 60, Fat Composition: 5g, Carb Compositions: 3g, Protein Composition: 1g, Total Sugar: 0g

COCONUT GOLDEN TEA

PREP.TIME: 5 min

COOK.TIME: 10 min

METHOD OF COOK.: Simmering

SERVES: 2

INGR: 2 C. water

- 1 tsp ground turmeric

- 1 Tbls coconut oil

- 1 pinch black pepper

- 1 Tbls heavy cream

- Erythritol or stevia to taste

PROC: Bring water to a boil

- Add turmeric and simmer for 10 min

- Stir in coconut oil, black pepper, heavy cream, and sweetener

TIPS: Add a teaspoon of grated ginger for extra zing

- Consume warm for best health benefits

N.V.: Caloric Content: 100, Fat Composition: 9g, Carb Compositions: 2g, Protein Composition: 0g, Total Sugar: 0g

HERBAL CHIA FRESCA

PREP.TIME: 5 min

COOK.TIME: 0 min

METHOD OF COOK.: Stirring

SERVES: 1

INGR: 1 C. brewed herbal tea (chilled)

- 1 Tbls chia seeds

- Juice of 1 lemon

- 1 tsp erythritol

PROC: Combine all ingredients in a glass and stir well

- Let sit for 5 min to allow chia seeds to swell

TIPS: Enjoy with a sprig of mint for a fresh taste

- Keep hydrated by turning this into your go-to morning refreshment

N.V.: Caloric Content: 50, Fat Composition: 3g, Carb Compositions: 5g, Protein Composition: 2g, Total Sugar: 0g

KETO MATCHA LATTE

PREP.TIME: 5 min

COOK.TIME: 0 min

METHOD OF COOK.: Blending

SERVES: 1

INGR: 1 tsp matcha powder

- 1 C. unsweetened almond milk

- 1 Tbls MCT oil

- Erythritol to taste

PROC: Heat almond milk until hot but not boiling

- Blend hot milk, matcha powder, MCT oil, and erythritol until frothy

TIPS: Experiment with adding a pinch of cinnamon or vanilla for variety

- Serve immediately for best flavor

N.V.: Caloric Content: 130, Fat Composition: 14g, Carb Compositions: 1g, Protein Composition: 2g, Total Sugar: 0g

ALMOND BUTTER COFFEE BOOSTER

PREP.TIME: 5 min

COOK.TIME: 0 min

METHOD OF COOK.: Blending

SERVES: 1

INGR: 1 C. brewed coffee

- 1 Tbls almond butter

- 1 Tbls coconut oil

- ¼ tsp cinnamon

- Erythritol to taste

PROC: Blend all ingredients until smooth and creamy

TIPS: Pour into a tall glass and sprinkle with a little unsweetened cocoa powder if desired

- Perfect for a mid-afternoon energy boost

N.V.: Caloric Content: 180, Fat Composition: 18g, Carb Compositions: 3g, Protein Composition: 3g, Total Sugar: 1g

10.   42-DAY MEAL PLAN

Embarking on a journey to transform your dietary habits can often feel like a daunting, overwhelming pursuit. However, with the right system in place — such as our structured 42-Day Meal Plan — the path becomes much clearer and achievable. This meal plan, crafted with precision and care, isn't just a strict schedule to follow; it is a guide, a confidante on your journey towards a healthier you.

Imagine having a roadmap that not only suggests the route but also ensures you have all the right tools for the journey. That's what this 42-day guide represents. It's meticulously designed to incorporate a variety of meals that align with your low Carb Composition, high Protein Composition dietary goals while being mindful of your time constraints and family dynamics. Each recipe is chosen to transform everyday ingredients into delicious, nutritional gold without requiring long hours in the kitchen.

Through this guide, you will discover that each week is balanced with flavors and nutrition. We start simple, with meals that build the foundation of your diet, and gradually introduce more diverse dishes to enhance your palette and prevent monotony. Sundays are your 'prep days'—a concept that will ease much of your weekly load, allowing you to enjoy wholesome homemade meals even on your busiest days.

Furthermore, this meal plan will serve as your companion, ensuring that you remain motivated with varied and delicious meal options that prevent boredom, a common challenge in maintaining a dietary regimen. The plan isn't just about losing weight or building muscle; it's designed to usher in a new outlook on food, how you prepare it, and how you enjoy it.

Whether you're cooking for one or feeding a family, these next 42 days will reshape your approach to meal times, ushering in lasting changes that go beyond mere physical health improvements to nurturing a joyous, rewarding relationship with your meals. Here's to setting the foundation of good health and excited taste buds!

DAY	BREAKFAST	LUNCH	SNACK	DINNER
1	Zucchini & Feta Frittata	Smoked Salmon Avocado Salad	Chia Seed & Coconut Energy Bites	Zesty Lime Shrimp and Avocado Salad
2	Almond Butter Pancakes	Mediterranean Tuna & Olive Salad	Smoked Salmon Cucumber Rolls	Beef and Broccoli Stir-Fry
3	Greek Yogurt Parfait	Chicken Caesar Espuma	Avocado Lime Mousse	Garlic Butter Shrimp with Zoodles
4	Cocoa-Almond Protein Composition Smoothie	Creamy Coconut Chicken Soup	Herbed Yogurt Cheese Balls	Cauliflower Steak with Almond Pesto

5	Turkey and Spinach Omelette	Steak and Arugula Salad	Sundried Tomato & Feta Hummus	Salmon with Creamy Dill Sauce
6	Vanilla Chai Protein Composition Shake	Broccoli & Cheddar Soup	Lemon Chia Seed Protein Composition Bars	Spicy Turkey Lettuce Wraps
7	Smoked Salmon Avocado Boats	Buffalo Chicken Salad	Kicked-Up Cottage Cheese Dip	Balsamic Glazed Beef Tenderloin
8	Avocado & Egg Breakfast Bowl	Chicken Zoodle Soup	Raspberry Coconut Protein Composition Pudding	Lemon Butter Scallops
9	Berry Silken Tofu Smoothie	Zesty Chicken Caesar Wrap	Turkey & Spinach Pinwheels	Herb-Crusted Salmon with Dijon Sauce
10	Chia and Blueberry Protein Composition Pancakes	Mediterranean Chickpea Salad	Vanilla Coconut Chia Pudding	Stuffed Chicken Breast with Spinach and Feta
11	Pumpkin Pie Protein Composition Shake	Egg Salad Lettuce Wrap	Pistachio & Cranberry Protein Composition Squares	Herb-Crusted Rack of Lamb
12	Smoked Salmon Scramble	Tofu and Edamame Salad Bowl	Basil Pesto Ricotta Dip	Prosciutto-Wrapped Cod with Lemon Cream Sauce
13	Avocado Green Tea Smoothie	Spicy Tomato & Tuna Stew	Herbed Goat Cheese Spread	Lemon Garlic Butter Flank Steak
14	Mocha Protein Composition Frappe	Spicy Shrimp & Tomato Bisque	Almond Butter and Chia Seed Spread	Mediterranean Shrimp Skillet
15	Coconut Almond Porridge	Beef and Horseradish Cream Wrap	Peanut Butter Protein Composition Truffles	Spicy Grilled Tofu with Avocado Salsa
16	Pepperoni and Egg Breakfast Pizza	Salmon and Cream Cheese Bagel	Chocolate Hazelnut Protein Composition Bites	Pork Chops with Apple Cider Vinegar Sauce
17	Tropical Turmeric Protein Composition Smoothie	Egg Salad Lettuce Wrap	Avocado and Lime Crema	Garlic Parmesan Crusted Chicken
18	Savory Chorizo Egg Cups	Beef and Arugula Salad	Smoked Salmon Pâté	Seared Scallops with Cauliflower Puree
19	Savory Turkey and Spinach Frittata	Broccoli & Cheddar Soup	Lemon Poppy Seed Protein Composition Bars	Cauliflower Steak with Almond Pesto
20	Berry Basil Blast Smoothie	Turkey Ranch Club	Almond Joy Protein Composition Shake	Chicken Piccata with Capers

21	Pumpkin Pie Protein Composition Shake	Spicy Tofu Wrap with Avocado	Chocolate Walnut Espresso Cookies	Lemon Garlic Shrimp Stir-Fry
22	Almond Butter Pancakes	Smoked Salmon Avocado Salad	Peanut Butter Protein Composition Truffles	Herb-Crusted Salmon with Dijon Sauce
23	Vanilla Chai Protein Composition Shake	Mediterranean Chickpea Salad	Turkey & Spinach Pinwheels	Lemon Butter Scallops
24	Avocado & Egg Breakfast Bowl	Chicken Caesar Espuma	Kicked-Up Cottage Cheese Dip	Balsamic Glazed Beef Tenderloin
25	Zucchini & Feta Frittata	Creamy Coconut Chicken Soup	Herbed Yogurt Cheese Balls	Stuffed Chicken Breast with Spinach and Feta
26	Pumpkin Pie Protein Composition Shake	Beef and Horseradish Cream Wrap	Lemon Chia Seed Protein Composition Bars	Garlic Parmesan Crusted Chicken
27	Chia and Blueberry Protein Composition Pancakes	Zesty Chicken Caesar Wrap	Smoked Salmon Pâté	Seared Scallops with Cauliflower Puree
28	Smoked Salmon Scramble	Spicy Tomato & Tuna Stew	Vanilla Coconut Chia Pudding	Prosciutto-Wrapped Cod with Lemon Cream Sauce
29	Greek Yogurt Parfait	Tofu and Edamame Salad Bowl	Basil Pesto Ricotta Dip	Herb-Crusted Rack of Lamb
30	Cocoa-Almond Protein Composition Smoothie	Broccoli & Cheddar Soup	Raspberry Coconut Protein Composition Pudding	Pork Chops with Apple Cider Vinegar Sauce
31	Mocha Protein Composition Frappe	Steak and Arugula Salad	Chocolate Hazelnut Protein Composition Bites	Spicy Grilled Tofu with Avocado Salsa
32	Berry Silken Tofu Smoothie	Turkey Ranch Club	Pistachio & Cranberry Protein Composition Squares	Lemon Garlic Butter Flank Steak
33	Coconut Almond Porridge	Egg Salad Lettuce Wrap	Herbed Goat Cheese Spread	Cauliflower Steak with Almond Pesto
34	Avocado Green Tea Smoothie	Mediterranean Tuna & Olive Salad	Sundried Tomato & Feta Hummus	Zesty Lime Shrimp and Avocado Salad
35	Pepperoni and Egg Breakfast Pizza	Buffalo Chicken Salad	Lemon Poppy Seed Protein Composition Bars	Beef and Broccoli Stir-Fry
36	Vanilla Chai Protein Composition Shake	Chicken Zoodle Soup	Almond Joy Protein Composition Shake	Spicy Turkey Lettuce Wraps

37	Turkey and Spinach Omelette	Smoked Salmon Avocado Salad	Chia Seed & Coconut Energy Bites	Salmon with Creamy Dill Sauce
38	Savory Turkey and Spinach Frittata	Mediterranean Chickpea Salad	Chocolate Walnut Espresso Cookies	Garlic Butter Shrimp with Zoodles
39	Cocoa-Almond Protein Composition Smoothie	Tofu and Edamame Salad Bowl	Smoked Salmon Cucumber Rolls	Herb-Crusted Salmon with Dijon Sauce
40	Pumpkin Pie Protein Composition Shake	Mediterranean Tuna & Olive Salad	Avocado Lime Mousse	Seared Scallops with Cauliflower Puree
41	Smoked Salmon Scramble	Spicy Shrimp & Tomato Bisque	Raspberry Coconut Protein Composition Pudding	Garlic Parmesan Crusted Chicken
42	Almond Butter Pancakes	Zesty Chicken Caesar Wrap	Basil Pesto Ricotta Dip	Lemon Butter Scallops

OVERCOMING CHALLENGES

As we set sail on the transformative journey outlined in our 42-Day Meal Plan, it's crucial to anchor ourselves, not just in the excitement of new beginnings but also in a steadfast understanding of potential challenges that might arise. Knowing how to navigate these challenges can be the difference between a fleeting attempt and a sustained lifestyle change.

One of the foremost challenges we face when adopting a new dietary plan is dealing with our body's initial resistance to change. As creatures of habit, our bodies and minds may initially rebel against new routines, especially ones that alter our diet so significantly. You might find yourself dealing with cravings, both physical and psychological. The key here is to anticipate these cravings and not let them derail you. Recognize them for what they are — not imperatives that must be obeyed but mere suggestions that can be acknowledged and then set aside.

Another hurdle often encountered is the perceived lack of time. In a world where the pace of life only seems to quicken, carving out chunks of time to plan, prepare, and cook meals can seem daunting, if not impossible. However, like any worthwhile endeavor, it requires investing time to reap the benefits in the long run. Perhaps it involves waking up a bit earlier or using time-saving meal prep strategies. Remember, the time you invest in preparing healthy meals is saved down the line — less time feeling sluggish, less time at medical appointments, and more time enjoying robust health.

Social gatherings and dining out can pose significant challenges, making you feel out of place or even isolated due to your dietary choices. Armed with a strong understanding of why you chose this path, you can navigate these situations with confidence. Be prepared with polite, concise explanations for your choices, if questioned, or bring your delicious creations to share, showcasing how nutritious can also be delicious.

Moreover, the sheer volume of dietary advice circulating in the public sphere can be overwhelming and often contradictory. This inundation can make sticking to a chosen path feel precarious. My advice? Choose your sources carefully, trust in the plan you've started, and remember why you started on this path.

Emotional eating is a major challenge, especially under stress, when the comfort of food seems like an easy solace. Here, it's crucial to develop other coping mechanisms for stress, which do not involve food. Whether it's meditation, taking a walk, or immersing yourself in a hobby that absorbs you completely, finding alternative relief methods can help maintain your dietary course when emotions run high.

As days turn into weeks, even the most determined may find their motivation waning. Always keep your goals in sight, and remind yourself why you began. Keeping a journal of not just what you eat, but how you feel physically and emotionally, can serve as a powerful motivational tool by highlighting the progress you've made, often in areas you hadn't anticipated.

Weight loss plateaus or periods where muscle gain seems to stagnate are perhaps among the most frustrating experiences when you're committed to a set meal plan. It's essential to understand that plateaus do not mean failure. They are a natural part of any weight loss journey. When you encounter a plateau, take it as a signal to reassess: perhaps it's time to spice up your meals a bit, adjust your macronutrient ratios, or change your exercise routine. Having flexible strategies within your meal plan can be crucial here.

In all these trials, the dual qualities of perseverance and flexibility are your best tools. Keep pushing forward, but not rigidly so. Adapt and adopt — tweak meal timings, switch up your recipe choices or even meal composition to suit your evolving needs. A plan is a guide, not a gospel. It's here to serve you and can be modified as you learn more about what works best for your body and lifestyle.

Navigating towards a healthier lifestyle is seldom without its share of challenges, but it's also filled with opportunities for growth, learning, and ultimately, a greater sense of well-being. By tuning into the body's needs, acknowledging and preparing for possible setbacks, embracing the community for support, and making adjustments as needed, not only will the journey on this 42-Day Meal Plan be smoother, but it can also become a sustainable, enjoyable way of life. As always, the most profound transformations are those we guide patiently and persistently, with a clear vision and a plan adaptable enough to navigate real life's complex ebbs and flows.

HANDLING CRAVINGS

It's a quiet evening. You've done well all day sticking to your high-Protein Composition, low-Carb Composition meals. Suddenly, there it is—the craving. A whisper perhaps for something sweet, or a shout from within for a slice of freshly baked bread. Cravings are not just whims; they're complex interactions of biology, environment, and psychology that can challenge even the most disciplined eater.

To handle cravings effectively, it's essential first to understand them. Cravings are often your body's way of telling you it needs something—it could be more energy, certain nutrients, or even an emotional fulfillment. However, not all cravings are created equal. Sometimes they stem from habits, like wanting a crunchy snack during your nightly TV show, or a response to emotional needs, such as comfort or a reward.

Strategies to Outsmart Cravings

Mindful Eating: Start with mindfulness. When a craving hits, pause. Question whether you are hungry or just reacting out of habit or emotion. Give yourself a moment to consider what your body needs. If you feel genuinely hungry, choose a wholesome snack that aligns with your dietary goals. If it's emotional, acknowledge the feeling and decide consciously how best to address it without diverting from your path.

Balanced Meals: Ensure your meals are balanced with enough Protein Compositions, healthy Fat Compositions, and fiber. This balance helps stabilize blood Total Sugar levels, which can prevent spikes and dips that lead to cravings. For instance, starting the day with a high-Protein Composition breakfast can reduce the desire for snacking on less desirable options later in the day.

Adequate Hydration: Thirst can often masquerade as hunger. Keeping hydrated throughout the day can help stave off unwarranted cravings. Sometimes, a refreshing glass of water is all it takes to push through a craving.

Healthy Alternatives: Keep healthy alternatives handy. Instead of reaching for chips, why not try a handful of nuts? Instead of ice cream, maybe a bowl of Greek yogurt with nuts and a bit of honey? Prepare these alternatives during your meal prep time so that they are as convenient as any processed snack.

While it's important to manage cravings realistically by occasional indulgences, make clever substitutions where possible. Love soda? Try sparkling water with a wedge of lemon. Craving chocolate? Opt for a small piece of dark chocolate that's low in Total Sugar but high in cocoa.

Your environment has a robust influence on what you eat. If your pantry and refrigerator are stocked with junk food, your cravings get an ally, making resistance tougher. Modify your environment to suit your goals. Make it a point to shop consciously—avoiding aisles full of processed foods and instead focusing on the whole, fresh ingredients that make up your meal plan.

Often, cravings are tied to our emotional state. Stress, boredom, sadness, and even joy can push us towards eating. Developing strategies to manage your emotional triggers can be crucial. Meditation, deep breathing exercises, or even a quick walk can provide an alternative release for these emotions.

Lack of sleep adjusts hormone levels in ways that increase cravings. Ensuring you get a regular, satisfying sleep each night can help stabilize these hormones, decreasing the frequency and intensity of cravings.

Each time you handle a craving successfully, take a moment to reflect on what worked. Keeping a note of these situations and your actions builds an arsenal of strategies that you can deploy as needed. If you succumb to a craving, don't be harsh on yourself. Reflect on why it happened and plan how you might handle a similar situation better next time.

Remember, you're not alone in this. Sharing your goals and struggles with friends or family members, or even a support group, can give you extra strength to push through the tough times. Knowing that others are rooting for you or are in the same boat can provide both comfort and motivation.

Cravings are a natural part of changing dietary habits, but with time, they diminish in intensity and frequency. The body's amazing adaptability means that tastes and preferences can evolve, helping you not only manage but eventually forget old unhealthy cravings. Patience and perseverance, supported by strategies like these, can transform temporary resistance into lasting success.

DEALING WITH PLATEAUS

Imagine you're on a scenic train journey; you've passed several beautiful stations with much excitement and progress. Suddenly, your train halts unexpectedly. You wait, a bit puzzled, wondering why the journey's paused. This is much like experiencing a plateau in your dietary journey—a common, albeit frustrating, part of any health and fitness regimen.

Plateaus occur when, despite following your meal plans and fitness routines diligently, you suddenly stop seeing progress.

It could manifest as your weight stalling on the scale or your muscle gain not being as apparent. Understanding why plateaus happen and learning how to push past them can reenergize your commitment and help you continue making strides towards your goals.

In the simplest terms, a plateau is your body adapting to its new conditions. As you lose weight or build muscle, your body requires fewer Caloric Content to function than it did at your starting weight. Essentially, what worked at the beginning may not work midway as your body's metabolic needs have changed.

First, ensure that what you're experiencing is indeed a plateau. If it's been a few weeks without any change, then you're likely facing a plateau. Note, it's important to measure progress in more ways than just the scale. Consider how your clothes fit, energy levels, and overall health improvements.

Shifting Strategies

Adjusting Your Caloric Intake: Revisit your caloric needs which have likely decreased as you've lost weight. Adjust your meal plan slightly below your new maintenance Caloric Content to trigger further weight loss.

Intensify Your Workouts: If your routine has become comfortable, it's time to turn up the intensity. Incorporate more strength training or increase the weights you're working with. Changing your exercise routine can also shock your body into responsiveness.

Ensure Macronutrient Balance: Check if your Protein Composition, Fat Composition, and Carb Compositionohydrate intake are aligned with your current goals. Sometimes simply tweaking these ratios can jumpstart progress.

Hydration and Sleep: Never underestimate the power of water and sleep. Dehydration and sleep deprivation can masquerade as weight-loss plateaus by causing water retention and altering hormone levels that manage appetite and weight.

Stress Management: High stress can halt progress through its impact on cortisol levels which in turn can affect your body's ability to lose weight or gain muscle. Incorporating stress-reducing activities like yoga or mindfulness can be beneficial.

Tracking and Flexibility

Journaling: Keep a detailed food and exercise journal. Sometimes, 'invisible Caloric Content' sneak in, or we might overestimate the intensity of our workouts. A journal helps maintain transparency with oneself.

Flexibility in Approach: Be open to trying new methods. If low Carb Composition isn't working as well anymore, it might be time to alter your macronutrient intake or experiment with different types of dietary approaches like intermittent fasting.

During a plateau, your mental game needs to be strong. It's easy to feel discouraged and revert to old habits. This is the time to remind yourself of your achievements and the health benefits you've gained thus far. Setting new, small, achievable goals can also keep your spirits up.

Sometimes, you might do everything right and still face a plateau. This is when it might be beneficial to consult with a dietitian or a trainer. Getting professional guidance can lend new perspectives and strategies that you might not have considered.

Lastly, remember that each step, even a halted one, is a part of a larger journey towards health. Patience, resilience, and adaptability are your best allies. Celebrate the distance covered, learn from the stillness of a plateau, and equip yourself to move forward with even greater wisdom. After all, it's these challenges that make the journey towards health and fitness all the more satisfying when you look back.

STAYING MOTIVATED

Embarking on a journey toward a healthier lifestyle is much like planting a garden. It requires patience, persistence, and most of all, continuous motivation to tend to it day after day. The 42-Day Meal Plan is your gardening schedule, but staying motivated through this plan and beyond is vital for harvesting the full benefits of your efforts. Keeping motivation high can be challenging, especially when progress seems slow or distractions arise.

Start by understanding the deeper reasons behind your desire to change. Is it to feel better, to be able to play with your kids without getting winded, or perhaps to manage a health condition? Aligning your dietary goals with your core values provides a reservoir of motivation that you can dip into when your energy wanes.

The old saying "Rome wasn't built in a day" holds true for dietary transitions as well. Setting large, long-term goals can be inspiring, but it's the small, daily achievements that pave the path to success. Break your goals into manageable, bite-sized pieces. Celebrate every small victory to keep the motivational momentum going. For example, instead of focusing solely on weight loss, set goals for daily hydration, weekly meal prepping, or the number of Protein Composition-rich meals consumed per week.

Picture yourself achieving your goals. How will you feel? What will change in your daily life? Visualization is a powerful tool for maintaining motivation. It allows you to glimpse the rewards of your hard work, making them more tangible and attainable.

Positive reinforcement also plays a crucial role in staying motivated. Treat yourself with non-food rewards for meeting smaller goals.

Perhaps a new workout outfit, a day out in nature, or a new book can be your prize for sticking with your meal plan through the week.

No man, or woman, is an island—surrounding yourself with a community that supports your goals can significantly enhance your motivation. Whether it's family, friends, or online support groups, sharing the journey makes the load lighter and the journey more enjoyable. When you're feeling down or tempted to stray from your meal plan, a quick chat with a supportive friend can uplift your spirits and re-align your focus.

Every journey will have its bumps and setbacks; they are not a sign of failure but opportunities for learning. When you face a setback, reflect on what led to it and how it can be avoided in the future. Understanding and addressing the root causes of setbacks enhances your strategy and preparation, which boosts your confidence and motivation to continue.

Document your journey. Keeping a journal allows you to track not just what you eat and when you exercise, but also your emotional and physical health throughout the process. On days when motivation is lacking, looking back over your progress can provide a substantial motivational boost. Write down how you feel after eating well or completing a workout, and remind yourself of these positives when you feel inclined to skip a meal prep or indulge in unhealthy eating.

Be willing to adapt your strategies as you progress. If boredom sets in, try new recipes or experiment with different meals that still align with your dietary goals. Interrupting monotony can reignite your enthusiasm.

Expand your knowledge about nutritional health and cooking techniques. Understanding the science behind your diet or discovering delicious, diet-compliant recipes can reinforce your commitment and make your meal plan more enjoyable. The more you know, the more empowered you feel to make the right choices, which fuels ongoing motivation.

Spend time reflecting on how far you've come and the effort you've invested. Being mindful of your daily habits helps you maintain a conscious connection to your lifestyle choices. This daily affirmation of your commitment can push you through days of low energy or apparent stagnancy.

Finally, remember that motivation is not something you find or lose—it's something you create, day after day. It's built through consistent actions, a positive mindset, and a willingness to overcome the challenges that inevitably arise. By cultivating resilience and patience and celebrating every step forward, you keep the fires of motivation burning brightly, illuminating your path to a healthier, happier life.

11. CONCLUSION AND CONTINUING YOUR JOURNEY

As we draw near the conclusion of our transformative journey with the "Time-Saving Low Carb Composition High Protein Composition Cookbook," it's essential to reflect on the strides you've taken towards a healthier, vibrant self. Embracing a low-Carb Composition, high-Protein Composition diet isn't merely about following recipes—it's a commitment to nurturing your body and safeguarding your well-being against the hurried pace of modern life.

Imagine waking up each day feeling energized, muscle fibers firmed from nutritious fuel, Fat Composition trimmed through wise eating choices. This image is not an ephemeral daydream but a sustainable reality you can maintain through continued practice of our efficient cooking methods and insightful meal planning. As with any endeavor that improves quality of life, persistence is key. The transition you've embarked upon may have presented a steep learning curve initially, but each day paved the pathway toward becoming more adept at selecting the right foods and mastering quick, wholesome meal preparation.

Your journey doesn't end here. Rather, think of this as a base camp. Ahead lies the continuous climb, filled with opportunities to refine and diversify your dietary habits. Each meal is a chance to explore new flavors and textures, to convert the unassuming grocery store run into a rewarding treasure hunt for the freshest, most nutritious ingredients. The skills you've developed—the quick chops, the instinctual measurements, the keen eye for Carb Composition counts—are tools that will serve you well as your culinary adventure evolves.

One of the most inspiring aspects of this dietary shift is the profound impact it has not just on the individual, but on your family and friends too. Sharing a quick, Protein Composition-rich breakfast with your family sets everyone up for success. It's about more than the meals; it's about the shared moments and the lifestyle you model—a ripple effect of health that extends through your loved ones. Welcoming guests with impressive low-Carb Composition dishes that burst with flavor challenges the myth that healthy eating is dull or limiting. You're not just feeding people; you're inspiring them, showing that good health and gourmet pleasure are not mutually exclusive.

However, every journey encounters its storms. You might find yourself at a plateau in weight loss, or perhaps facing the temptation of high-Carb Composition treats during holiday seasons. Here, your newfound resilience shines brightest; these moments are not setbacks but opportunities to strengthen resolve. Recall the delicious satisfaction of the meals you've mastered; let that motivate you through challenging episodes. Learning to prepare quick, appealing recipes that align with your diet is your armor and your comfort—it's what makes the path sustainable, even enjoyable.

Remember, too, that perfection is not the goal—consistency is. Flexibility in your approach can help you navigate through social gatherings and vacations, times when strict adherence to a dietary regimen can be difficult. Applying the principles of high-Protein Composition, low-Carb Composition eating in a way that suits each unique situation reveals not just a mastery of the diet, but an adaptation of the lifestyle.

Looking forward, consider how this book might remain a tool in your arsenal. The 42-day meal plan, the high Protein Composition smoothies, the quick weeknight meals—revisit them periodically, mixing and matching to suit your evolving tastes and nutritional needs.

The science of nutrition continually advances, and keeping abreast of these changes can help you adjust your diet to benefit from the latest research, ensuring that your routine stays as effective as it is gratifying.

Moreover, your journey might evolve into advocacy. As you share your stories of transformation and triumph, as you cook for friends and explain the rationale behind your food choices, you influence others. Each explanation about the benefits of a low-Carb Composition, high-Protein Composition diet, each shared meal of delicious, healthful food extends your impact, weaving your personal successes into the larger tapestry of community health improvement.

As we part ways in this book, my hope is that your kitchen becomes a haven of health, a place where the low-Carb Composition and high-Protein Composition foods you prepare continue to bring vitality and joy not just to your plate, but also to your life. Keep this book close—let it be a friendly voice guiding you through the highs and the lows, reminding you that with each meal, you're crafting not just food, but a legacy of health. Your path doesn't end; it widens, inviting you to tread further, explore deeper, and live fully.

12.   MEASUREMENT CONVERSION TABLE

Volume Equivalents (Liquid)

US Standard	US Standard (ounces)	Metric (approximate)
2 tablespoons	1 fl. oz.	30 mL
¼ cup	2 fl. oz.	60 mL
half cup	4 fl. oz.	120 mL
1 cup	8 fl. oz.	240 mL
1 half cups	12 fl. oz.	355 mL
2 cups or 1 pint	16 fl. oz.	457 mL
4 cups or 1 quart	32 fl. oz.	1 L
1 gallon	128 fl. oz.	4 L

Volume Equivalents (Dry)

US Standard	Metric (approximate)
1/8 teaspoon	0.5 mL
¼ teaspoon	1 mL
half teaspoon	2 mL
¾ teaspoon	4 mL
1 teaspoon	5 mL
1 tablespoon	15 mL
¼ cup	59 mL
1/3 cup	79 mL
half cup	118 mL
2/3 cup	156 mL
¾ cup	177 mL
1 cup	235 mL
2 cups or 1 pint	475 mL
3 cups	700 mL
4 cups or 1 quart	1 L

Oven Temperatures

Fahrenheit (F)	Celsius (C) (approximate)
250°F	120°C
300°F	150°C
325°F	165°C
350°F	180°C
375°F	190°C
400°F	200°C
425°F	220°C
450°F	230°C

Weight Equivalents

US Standard	Metric (approximate)
1 tablespoon	15 g
half ounce	15 g
1 ounce	30 g
2 ounces	60 g
4 ounces	115 g
8 ounces	225 g
12 ounces	340 g
16 ounces or 1 pound or 1 lb	455 g

Made in the USA
Las Vegas, NV
14 December 2024